Plants That Poison

Plants
That Poison

An Illustrated Guide to Plants Poisonous to Man

by ERVIN M. SCHMUTZ, Ph.D.
and LUCRETIA BREAZEALE HAMILTON

with illustrations by Lucretia Breazeale Hamilton

NORTHLAND PRESS / FLAGSTAFF, ARIZONA

Contents

Illustrations

Foreword

The development of an interest in eating natural foods and various plant parts, as well as the worry of mothers whose young children put things into their mouths, has produced a need for a book of caution about the dangers involved with poisonous or potentially poisonous plants. This book ably fulfills that need for the southwestern United States.

Dr. Schmutz, already well versed in poisonous plant literature through his publication *Livestock-Poisoning Plants of Arizona,* has assembled an impressive list of native and cultivated plants which grow in the Southwest and can cause severe distress.

The artist, Mrs. Lucretia Hamilton, has illustrated many publications on southwestern plants and draws with the necessary accuracy and detail to permit the ready recognition of each species.

The publication of *Plants That Poison* fills a void that has grown greater and more obvious with the increased development of the Southwest.

Charles T. Mason, Jr.
Curator of the Herbarium
University of Arizona

Acknowledgments

The authors are indebted to Dr. Charles T. Mason, Jr., Curator of the Herbarium at the University of Arizona, for review and evaluation of the manuscript, for advice on the taxonomy and distribution of plants, and for his cooperation in obtaining plant mounts for line drawings; to Dr. Albert L. Picchioni, Head of the Department of Pharmacology and Toxicology and Director of the Poison Control Center, for information and references on poisonous plants and their symptoms; to Dr. Alan D. Barreuther, in the Department of Pharmaceutical Sciences and the Poison Control Center, for review of and suggestions on the manuscript; to Dr. Wayburn S. Jeter, Head of the Department of Microbiology and Director of the Cellular Immunology Laboratory, for consultations and review of the section on botulism; to Dr. Robert W. Hoshaw, Department of Ecology and Evolutionary Biology, for review of and suggestions on the section on algae; and to Drs. Robert L. Gilbertson and Roger L. Caldwell, Department of Plant Pathology, for consultations and review of the sections on fungi.

Appreciation is also expressed to the University of Arizona Herbarium, the University of Texas Herbarium, Mr. Louis P. Hamilton, Mr. Thomas P. Harlan, and all other persons, businesses, and agencies who collected, granted, or loaned plants or plant mounts used in making illustrations.

We are also deeply grateful to the University of Arizona for the loan of many line drawings used in this publication and to the University of Arizona Press for permission to use a number of line drawings previously published in an *Illustrated Guide to Arizona Weeds* by K. F. Parker, *Trees and Shrubs of the Southwestern Deserts* by L. Benson and R. A. Darrow, and *Livestock-Poisoning Plants of Arizona* by E. M. Schmutz, B. N. Freeman, and R. E. Reed.

Thanks are also expressed to the personnel of Northland Press for their cooperation and suggestions on the format, composition, and style of this book and for effecting its publication.

EMS
LBH

This Book and How to Use It

The use of plants by man for food, clothing, hunting, and shelter has always been an essential part of his existence. In addition, plants have been used as medicines, in religious ceremonies, and for poisonings in political intrigues and executions. In modern times there is a growing interest in plants for use as "natural foods," for hallucinogenic experimentation and use, for ornamentation and landscaping, and for medicines and drugs.

While plants can be useful, they may also be harmful, causing addiction, sickness, and death. This book is designed to provide information on the identification and distribution of poisonous plants, the effects of their accidental or intentional use, and the identity and location of toxins when known. Noxious chemicals present in plants are alkaloids, glycosides, resins, alcohols, phenols, phytotoxins, and oxalates. A glossary of technical terms precedes the index of the book.

Included are plants of the southwestern United States and northwestern Mexico which have specific or multiple poisonous substances that cause toxic reactions, illness, or death in humans. Strictly hay-fever and dermatitis-producing plants have been omitted. A few relatively nontoxic plants with poisonous reputations are included for clarification.

Often, these same poisonous plants (in properly prescribed, relatively small amounts) are used for medicinal purposes to cure illnesses, relieve pain, control bodily functions, and to kill infectious organisms.

Plants covered are native and introduced wild plants, cultivated crops, ornamental and garden plants, and house plants. Each plant is identified by common and scientific names followed by a brief description of the plant and its distribution, the toxic parts and poisonous principles, symptoms of poisoning, and pertinent comments. Line drawings are included for identification of most plants. General sections on prevention and treatment are included, plus a table of contents, glossary, and index.

The plants are arranged in the text in alphabetical order by the most accepted common name. Other common and scientific names are also included, and plants can be located by these names through the index. Some plants, like mushrooms and poppies, are listed together by species for quick comparison. Plants unfamiliar to the reader may be identified by the line drawings. The fact that a plant is not included in this book does not imply that it is not poisonous, since the poisonous properties of many plants are unknown. There are undoubtedly some poisonous plants present in the Southwest without our knowledge and others which will appear in the area in the future.

Precautions and Cautions

Fortunately, most poisonous plants must be eaten in relatively large amounts to be toxic to adults. Generally, poisonous plants have an unpleasant taste and normally will not be chewed or eaten in sufficient amounts to cause serious illness. However, curious children or experimenting adults may eat large amounts with disastrous results. In the case of small children or situations in which plants are extremely poisonous, even small amounts (especially of seeds) can cause serious illness or death. Under these conditions, the best approach to the poisonous plant problem is prevention. The first step is to identify the poisonous and dermatitis-producing plants in your home, garden, work, and recreation areas, and learn to live with them. The next step is to become familiar with the effects they produce so that poisonings can be readily recognized and treated.

Another precaution is to teach your family, especially children, not to eat seeds, fruits, bulbs, or tubers; to abstain from drinking tea made from leaves or sucking nectar from flowers; to avoid breathing the smoke; and not to take medical preparations made from parts of any known poisonous or unknown plant. Also, keep plants that are known to be or even suspected of being poisonous out of reach of infants.

Heating or cooking plants in water removes many poisons, but don't bet your life on it.

Birds and pets eat some berries and fruits poisonous to humans, seemingly without harm; consequently, what they eat cannot be used as a guide to non-poisonous plants. However, many plants poisonous to humans are also poisonous to pets.

Not all plants with milky juice are poisonous. On the other hand, so many plants with milky juice are toxic that it should be considered a signal for caution.

Some herbal and natural food stores carry toxic herbs safe to use in proper amounts. Use of these herbs should be made with caution.

Not all plant parts are equally toxic nor are toxic plants always poisonous. The hazard varies with the particular type and sex of the plant, the stage of growth, the season of the year, the amount eaten, and the condition, age, and size of the person eating the plant.

Many poisonous and nonpoisonous plants that cause teratogenic (malforming) and carcinogenic (cancerous) effects in animals may cause similar effects in humans.

Most poisonous plants are harmful only when eaten. However, some plants (especially the sap) can produce caustic effects to the skin, injury to the eyes and/or dermatitis. In a few cases the poison can be absorbed directly through the skin or through cuts in the skin.

The use of plants for self-medication or professional prescription increases the opportunity for and danger of poisoning by plants due to (1) the additional number of persons exposed to the poisons and (2) the greater danger of overdose due to the concentration of the toxin in the medication.

The fact that plants are poisonous doesn't necessarily mean that they should be destroyed or that a law should be passed to ban their use. The principal hazard is not in the plants themselves but in our unfamiliarity with the plants, their properties, and uses. Without poisonous plants the world would be deprived of many of its life-saving drugs, popular food plants, beautiful ornamentals, and useful insecticides.

Aid for Persons Poisoned by Plants

Time is the most important factor when treating persons poisoned by plants. The most urgent consideration is how to remove the toxic substance from the system before it is absorbed. Your best help is a physician. Therefore, THE FIRST STEP IS TO CALL A PHYSICIAN IMMEDIATELY.

You can help most by being able to identify or describe the plant and plant parts eaten, when and how much was eaten, and the symptoms you have observed. If available, collect a sample of the plant and take it with you for identification or verification. If there is a question about which plant was eaten, take samples of plants in the area, but don't spend much time to do it. Include leaves, flowers, and fruits, if available. Use gloves or instruments to avoid getting sap on your hands. Sap is often the most toxic part of the plant and may cause poisoning or dermatitis. It is also important to keep plant parts taken from the mouth of the patient or present in the vomit or stools.

Since time is such a critical factor, keep telephone numbers handy for your physician, hospital, poison control center, and rescue unit.

IF A PHYSICIAN IS NOT AVAILABLE, GIVE FIRST AID AND PROMPTLY TRANSPORT PATIENT TO A HOSPITAL.

The basic principles for first aid to persons poisoned by plants are to dilute the poison with water, remove the poison from the system, and/or wash it off the skin.

Dilute the poison by giving one or two glassfuls of plain water.

If plants are swallowed in toxic quantities, induce vomiting, but not if the patient is unconscious, is having convulsions, or has already vomited. If there is a possibility that the poison swallowed is a strong acid, alkali, or petroleum distillate rather than a poisonous plant, do not induce vomiting.

To induce vomiting give one tablespoonful (½ ounce) of syrup of ipecac for a child one year of age or older in one or more cups of water. Repeat once more (but only once) if vomiting doesn't occur within 20 minutes. If no ipecac is available, induce vomiting by tickling the back of the throat with a spoon handle, finger, or other blunt object. The use of warm salt water to induce vomiting is not recommended because of the danger to children of poisoning by the salt water itself. Don't waste time waiting for vomit but transport the patient promptly to a medical facility. After vomiting has occurred or the stomach emptied give 1 to 2 tablespoonfuls of activated charcoal to absorb any remaining poison.

If the plant causes dermatitis, wash affected parts promptly (preferably within 10 minutes) with a large amount of water, using strong soap if available.

Plants That Poison

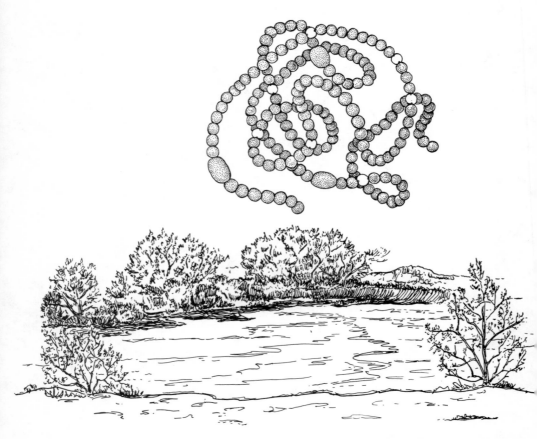

ALGAE   Toxic algae are common in quiet, nutrient-rich warm waters throughout the world. Filaments of *Anabaena,* a common toxic algal genus, are shown above.

ALGAE

Blue-green Algae
pondscum, plankton (Cyanophyta division)

DESCRIPTION AND DISTRIBUTION: Blue-green algae occur world-wide. They are microscopic green plants that form unicells, colonies, and filaments in or on any body of water. Poisoning results only when certain species grow rapidly in fertile waters in hot, sunny weather and form a scum or bloom on or in the upper layers of the water. Dangerous waters usually look like thin blue or gray paint. Types of algae which form filamentous mats on the surface of the ponds are not considered toxic.

TOXIC PARTS: Entire plant.

POISONING: Only certain species of blue-green algae are toxic. Several unknown toxic principles are involved. Persons may be poisoned by inhaling gas associated with algal growth, or by drinking or swimming in water covered with dense blooms of the toxic species. Pets, fish, and other animals are also susceptible. Some of the deaths associated with algal blooms may be due to botulism caused by clostridium bacteria found in the blooms. Also, allergenic reactions may be caused by inhaling the algae and by swimming in or swallowing contaminated water.

SYMPTOMS: Symptoms usually occur in 15 to 45 minutes, death within 1 to 24 hours. Symptoms are numbness of the face and tingling of the fingertips, nausea, vomiting, abdominal pain, diarrhea, prostration, muscular tremors, difficulty in breathing, bluish skin, general paralysis, convulsions, and death. In uncommon cases in which death doesn't occur rapidly, feces may become bloody; jaundice, dermatitis, and photosensitization may occur. If the patient survives the first 24 hours, chances for recovery are favorable.

COMMENTS: Another type of algal poisoning, which does not occur in the Southwest, is the "Red Tide" poisoning caused by dinoflagellate algae. This poisoning occurs commonly on the coasts and gulfs of the Atlantic and Pacific Oceans. Human poisoning and death can occur when these toxic algae are ingested directly or when fish or shellfish which have eaten the algae are in turn eaten by man.

AMARYLLIS   This species is charaterized by large, showy, brilliantly colored flowers and green strap-shaped leaves. The seed and seedpod are shown on the left, the bulb on the lower right.

ALMONDS

Bitter Almond
(Prunus dulcis var. amara)

Sweet Almond
(Prunus dulcis var. dulcis)

Almonds are small, cultivated broad-crowned trees in the rose family introduced from western Asia. They have long, narrow finely toothed leaves and white-to-pinkish flowers. The fruit is a soft- or hard-shelled nut. Sweet almonds are grown for their edible nuts, the inedible bitter almonds for the oil of bitter almond used in industry. Bitter almond seeds contain the poisonous compound amygdalin (a cyanogenetic glycoside) in quantity sufficient to cause poisoning; the sweet varieties are harmless. It is difficult, however, for even a botanist to separate the varieties. Fortunately, bitter almond is not commonly grown in this country.

AMARYLLIS

Amaryllis
Barbados-Lily *(Hippeastrum puniceum)* and other species

DESCRIPTION AND DISTRIBUTION: These plants are bulbous herbs of the amaryllis family introduced from tropical America and Africa. Leaves are basal and strap-shaped. Flowers are in clusters at the ends of hollow, leafless flower stalks. Flowers are showy, variegated red, pink, green and/or yellowish-white, and tubular with a flared opening. Seeds are produced in lobed capsules. Species are widely grown in the United States as house plants and in the Southwest as garden plants.

TOXIC PART: Bulbs.

POISONING: The bulbs of these plants are suspected of being poisonous and should be kept out of reach of small children.

SYMPTOMS: Nausea, vomiting, stomach pain, diarrhea, and respiratory paralysis.

COMMENT: The name *Amaryllis* has been applied to this species. However, recent literature indicates *Hippeastrum* is correct for this species while other species belong in *Amaryllis* (see Belladonna-Lily).

TUBER ANEMONE   This species is characterized by the dissected leaves, the solitary rose-colored flowers, the hairy seeds, and the tuberous rhizome that gives this southwestern **species** its name.

ANEMONES

Tuber Anemone
windflower *(Anemone tuberosa)* and other species

DESCRIPTION AND DISTRIBUTION: Anemones are native and cultivated perennial herbs of the crowfoot or buttercup family growing in
prairies and high mountains of the north temperate zone. Leaves are
more or less dissected, sometimes hairy, and often forming a cluster
below the flowers. Most of the flowers are solitary at the ends of seed
stalks and are white, yellow, rose, red, or purple in color. Fruits are
small, dry one-seeded capsules. In some species each fruit has a long
feathery tail.

TOXIC PARTS: Entire plant.

POISONING: The plants have long been suspected of being poisonous, but clear-cut proof is lacking. Ranunculin, which breaks down into
the toxic oil protoanemonin, is contained in these plants, making them
potentially dangerous.

SYMPTOMS: Burning of the mouth and skin, prickling sensation on
the skin, nervousness, nausea, vomiting, low blood pressure, depression, weak pulse, and convulsions.

COMMENTS: Protoanemonin is not a highly toxic substance and is
unstable. Upon drying it readily breaks down into the harmless substance anemonin. Anemones may also cause dermatitis in susceptible
persons. Japanese anemone *(Anemone hupehensis)* is a common cultivated species.

APPLE   Note the oval pointed leaves with saw-toothed edges and attractive flowers.
Crabapple is shown in the upper right, the delicious apple variety in the lower right.
An enlarged seed is in the center.

Apple
(Malus sylvestris)

DESCRIPTION AND DISTRIBUTION: Apple is a small cultivated tree in the rose family that was introduced from Europe and western Asia. Leaves are oval in shape and finely toothed. Flowers are white to pink, and the fruit is a fleshy yellow to red pome with several seeds in a core. Numerous varieties have been developed from the original wild apple. Several closely related, smaller-fruited species are known as crabapples.

TOXIC PARTS: Seeds, although leaves may also be cyanogenetic.

POISONING: The seeds of apples are cyanogenetic. Normally they are not eaten or at least not eaten in sufficient quantity to cause poisoning in humans. The classic exception referred to frequently in the literature is the man who liked apple seeds so much he saved a cupful and ate them all at once — with fatal results.

SYMPTOMS: Symptoms of cyanide poisoning which occur in rapid succession are giddiness, headache, heart palpitation, paralysis of the voice, difficulty in breathing, and unconsciousness. Later, nausea, vomiting, and convulsions may occur. A distinctive characteristic is the odor of almonds (benzaldehyde) on the breath or in the tissues of the body after death.

COMMENTS: An apple a day may keep the doctor away but not a cupful of apple seeds. The fleshy part of the fruit is harmless.

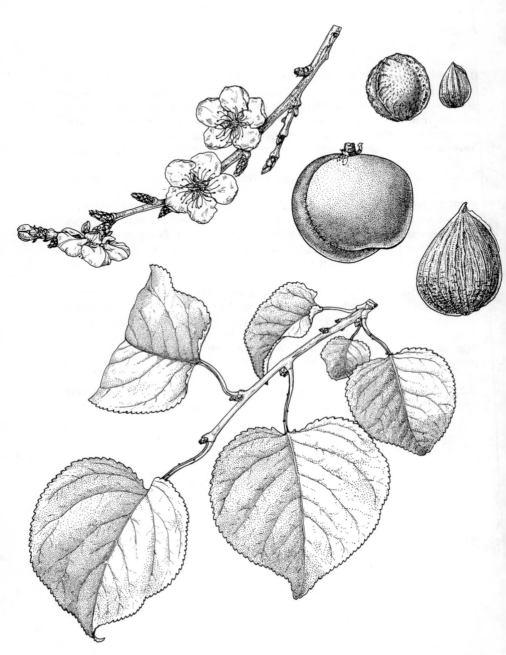

APRICOT   Note the heart-shaped leaves with saw-toothed edges, the fleshy short-stemmed fruit, the hard flattened seed, and the teardrop kernel (upper right).

Apricot
(Prunus armeniaca)

DESCRIPTION AND DISTRIBUTION: Apricot is a small cultivated tree in the rose family that was introduced from China. It has reddish bark and oval-shaped pointed leaves with saw-toothed edges. Flowers are pinkish or white and solitary. Fruit is medium-sized, round, smooth, and yellow with a very short stem. The stone (seed) is nearly smooth and somewhat flattened. The plant blooms early, before its leaves emerge; consequently, it is grown mostly in California and the Rocky Mountain states where late spring frosts are not severe.

TOXIC PARTS: Seeds and leaves.

POISONING: Like all members of the *Prunus* genus the plants contain cyanogenic glycosides which break down into hydrocyanic (prussic) acid upon hydrolysis. Children have been poisoned from eating the seeds.

SYMPTOMS: Dizziness, spasms, and coma. Also, headache, muscular weakness, nausea, vomiting, difficulty in breathing, and irregular heartbeat may occur.

COMMENTS: The controversial, reputedly cancer-curing drug laetrile is extracted from the seeds. Uncontrolled consumption of the whole seeds can be dangerous. The fleshy part of the fruit is edible.

HEARTLEAF ARNICA Conspicuous yellow flowers, heart-shaped leaves, bristly seeds, and underground rootstocks are characteristic of this species.

ARNICA

Heartleaf Arnica
(Arnica cordifolia)

DESCRIPTION AND DISTRIBUTION: Heartleaf arnica is a southwestern relative of the poisonous European mountain arnica *(Arnica montana)*. It is also suspected of being poisonous to humans. A low perennial herb in the sunflower family, it is found in the western mountains from Arizona and New Mexico to Alaska. The plants rise from underground rootstocks (stems). The heart-shaped basal leaves are larger than the stem leaves. The yellow-flowered composite heads are borne singly on long flower stalks. The fruit is a dry one-seeded fruit (achene) with a crown of bristles.

TOXIC PARTS: Flowers and roots.

POISONING: The toxin is a volatile oil. Danger of poisoning is greatest in children. Local applications may also cause dermatitis.

SYMPTOMS: Vomiting, diarrhea, drowsiness, respiratory distress, and coma, when eaten. Dermatitis symptoms are a severe skin irritation.

COMMENTS: There are no documented cases of poisoning of humans by arnica in the United States. Patients should recover after proper treatment without serious consequences. The tincture of arnica used in medicine is also derived from mountain arnica.

11

ASPARAGUS   The fleshy, scaly sprouts of the new shoots (left), the spreading foliage of the mature plant (center), the longitudinal sections of the separate female flower above and male below (upper right), the enlarged flower (lower right), and the round red berry and black triangular seed (lower center) characterize this important garden vegetable.

Asparagus

garden asparagus, common asparagus *(Asparagus officinalis)*

DESCRIPTION AND DISTRIBUTION: Asparagus is a tall hardy perennial herb in the lily family growing from underground rootstocks. Stems are simple, fleshy, scaly, and edible when young. Mature plants have many widely spreading, slender green branches. Leaves are small and scalelike; flowers are small, yellow or yellow green, and nodding; the fruits are red berries with few seeds. An introduction from the Mediterranean region, the common asparagus is cultivated for its fleshy shoots; other species are cultivated as ornamentals. Some have escaped in local areas.

TOXIC PARTS: Berries.

POISONING: The berries are suspected of poisoning humans, the mature plants of poisoning cattle.

SYMPTOMS: None documented.

COMMENTS: Poisoning of humans by asparagus is unlikely, but young plants frequently cause dermatitis.

AUTUMN-CROCUS   The narrow parallel-veined leaves growing from a bulb (right) and the colorful flowers (left) are characteristic of this attractive plant. The flowers and leaves appear separately — the flowers in the fall and the leaves in the spring.

Autumn-Crocus
meadow-saffron, naked-ladies *(Colchicum autumnale)*

DESCRIPTION AND DISTRIBUTION: Autumn-crocus is a stemless, bulbous herb in the lily family with long, narrow basal leaves. Flowers are white to purple, growing in clusters and blooming in the fall. Fruit is a splitting capsule. An introduction from the Mediterranean region, autumn-crocus is cultivated as an ornamental throughout the United States and has become naturalized in some areas.

TOXIC PARTS: Entire plant.

POISONING: The toxin is the alkaloid colchicine and related compounds. All parts of the plant are poisonous but the bulbs are the most toxic and most dangerous. However, children have been poisoned by eating the flowers. Poisoning also may occur from drinking milk produced by cows that have eaten the plants.

SYMPTOMS: When eaten, the plants cause a burning pain in the mouth, nausea, vomiting, diarrhea, depression of the respiratory function, muscular weakness, prostration, kidney failure, and circulatory collapse.

COMMENTS: Colchicine has limited medicinal use in preventing gout. It has been used extensively in genetic research to produce polyploids in plants and animals, and ingestion of colchicine during pregnancy may induce genetic change in humans.

BOTULISM Botulism poisoning usually occurs when improperly home-canned non-acid foods or meats are eaten without thorough boiling. The rod-like bacterial cells, spore-producing rods, and free spores are shown on the right.

BACTERIA

Botulism Bacteria

food-poisoning bacteria *(Clostridium botulinum)*

DESCRIPTION AND DISTRIBUTION: Botulism bacteria are anaerobic organisms commonly found in the soil that develop toxins in the absence of air. They are sometimes found in spoiled, home-canned, non-acid fruits and vegetables, such as beets, corn, or string beans, and in home-canned meats, marinated vegetables, and salted fish. They may also be found in commercially canned tuna or sausages.

TOXIC PART: Toxins excreted by botulism bacteria.

POISONING: The toxins are chemicals similar in nature to phytotoxins in other plants. Poisoning occurs when the contaminated foods are eaten without having been thoroughly boiled for 10 minutes. Six different types of toxins have been found and designated by the letters A through F. The majority of poisonings are due to toxin types A and E which are associated with inadequately processed vegetables and meats. This type of food spoilage is particularly dangerous because it is not always accompanied by the production of gas, strong odor, or an unusual taste that can be detected. Poisoning can also result from toxins absorbed through cuts in the skin. This toxin is reported to be the most potent poison known to man.

SYMPTOMS: Typical symptoms appear in 12 to 36 hours. They include a feeling of fatigue, vomiting, dizziness, headache, constipation, double vision, sensitivity to light, involuntary movement of the eyeball, constriction of the throat, swollen tongue, difficulty in breathing and swallowing, muscular weakness, and incoordination. In fatal cases death usually occurs in 3 to 6 days due to respiratory failure.

COMMENTS: Another type of food-poisoning is caused by *Clostridium perfringens.* This develops in meat and meat products (gravy, creamed chicken, stew, or soup) when stored at warm temperatures for several hours. Typical symptoms of diarrhea with abdominal pain develop 8 to 24 hours after ingestion of contaminated food. Nausea is common but vomiting is rare. Usually recovery occurs in 12 to 24 hours.

Another type of bacterial poisoning is silo-filler's disease. Forage fermenting in silos produces toxic gases, chiefly nitrogen dioxide and nitrogen tetroxide. The gases are yellow brown in color and, being heavier than air, collect in the silo or a room at the base of the silo. A few breaths of these gases will injure lung tissues, causing death.

17

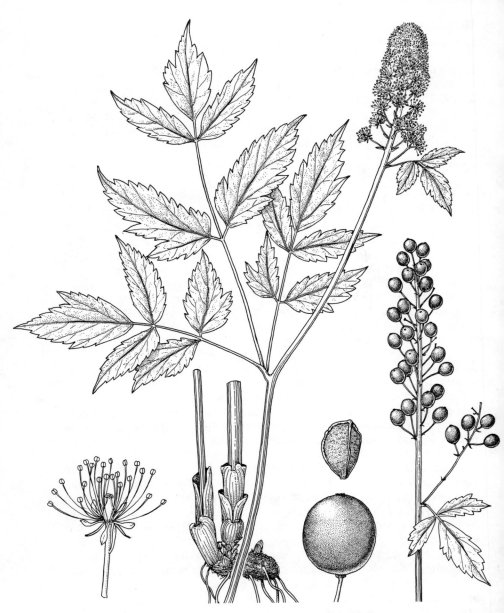

WESTERN BANEBERRY This species is characterized by the large divided leaves, the unusual flower (enlarged, lower left), and the clusters of red berries and seed (lower right).

BANEBERRY

Western Baneberry

red baneberry, snakeberry *(Actaea rubra* var. *arguta)*

DESCRIPTION AND DISTRIBUTION: Western baneberry is a tall perennial herb in the crowfoot or buttercup family with large, spreading, compound 3-foliate toothed leaves and thick root. Its white flowers and red berries with several seeds are borne in short terminal clusters. It is native to the forests and mountains of the western United States.

TOXIC PARTS: All parts, but mostly the berries, root, and sap.

POISONING: Toxic action is attributed to a glycoside or essential oil which causes severe inflammation of the stomach and intestines. As few as six berries can cause severe symptoms that last for hours.

SYMPTOMS: Severe stomach and abdominal pains, diarrhea, vomiting, dizziness, delirium, increased pulse, and circulatory failure. Fatalities have been reported but are rare.

COMMENT: Children are attracted to eating the bright red berries.

BEANS

Broad Bean

fava bean, horse bean, English bean *(Vicia faba)*

The seeds or pollen of this large bean can cause severe and even fatal hemolytic anemia (favism) in certain individuals of Italian, Greek, or Negro descent who inherit a deficiency in an essential enzyme (glucose-6-phosphate dehydrogenase).

Lima Bean

(Phaseolus limensis — also *Phaseolus lunatus)*

The colored plump varieties of this common food, usually grown in foreign countries, contain amounts of the cyanogenetic glycoside phaseolunatin that can cause cyanide poisoning. However, in the United States the danger of poisoning from these beans is remote since imported beans sold here must contain less than 0.01% cyanide, a safe level for consumption, and the beans grown in the United States are considered safe. In addition, cooking reduces the danger of poisoning.

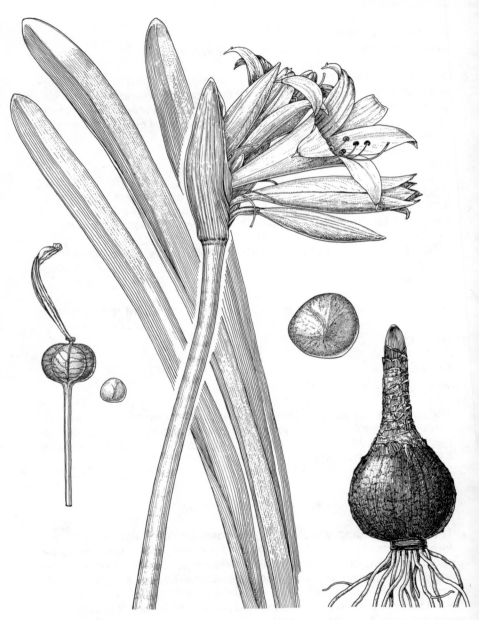

BELLADONNA-LILY The long naked flower stalk which appears before the leaves gives the plant one of its common names — naked-lady. The lobed capsule and seed are on the left, the seed (enlarged) and bulb on the right.

Belladonna-Lily

naked-lady, pink-lady, resurrection-lily *(Amaryllis belladonna)*

DESCRIPTION AND DISTRIBUTION: Belladonna-lily is a lily-like bulbous herb in the amaryllis family introduced from South Africa. Leaves are basal and strap-shaped. Flowers are clusters of large, attractive, rose-red to whitish lily-like flowers at the ends of long solid-stemmed stalks. Fruits are globose 3-lobed capsules containing oval seeds. Plants are cultivated in pots or planted outside in warmer climates.

TOXIC PART: Bulbs.

POISONING: The bulbs of belladonna-lily contain poisonous alkaloids that are dangerous, especially to children.

SYMPTOMS: Respiratory paralysis.

COMMENTS: Bulbs of other members of the amaryllis family — bloodlily *(Haemanthus* sp.), crinumlily *(Crinum* sp.), spiderlily *(Hymenocallis* sp.), and nerine *(Nerine* sp.) may also cause poisoning in humans. Another belladonna, the deadly nightshade *(Atropa belladonna),* an introduction from Europe, has occasionally escaped in the eastern United States and may be grown as an ornamental in the Southwest. It should be regarded as dangerous, especially to children, who are attracted to its black berries.

BIRD-OF-PARADISE BUSH This species is characterized by the large pinnately divided leaves, the colorful yellow flowers with long red stamens, the flat hairy seed pod (upper right), and the seed (enlarged, upper left) of this attractive ornamental shrub or small tree.

Bird-of-Paradise Bush

poinciana *(Caesalpinia gilliesii,* formerly *Poinciana gilliesii)*

DESCRIPTION AND DISTRIBUTION: Bird-of-paradise bush is an introduced, showy ornamental shrub or small tree in the legume family,
cultivated as a large potted plant or grown outside in the southern
United States and Hawaii. It is an occasional escape in the Southwest.
The leaves are pinnately divided, the flowers are yellow with long, colorful red filaments (stamens), and the pods are flat and legume-shaped.

TOXIC PARTS: Pods and seeds.

POISONING: The green seed pods cause serious stomach and intestinal irritation if eaten.

SYMPTOMS: Nausea, vomiting, and profuse diarrhea. Recovery occurs
in about 24 hours.

COMMENT: Another similar species, *Caesalpinia conzattii,* with yel-
lowish-red to brilliant-red flowers is probably also toxic.

BIRD-OF-PARADISE FLOWER The striking colorful flowers, the large banana-like leaf, and the bearded seed with the bright orange-colored tuft of hairs (enlarged, lower right) characterize this exotic ornamental shrub.

Bird-of-Paradise Flower
(Strelitzia reginae)

DESCRIPTION AND DISTRIBUTION: Bird-of-paradise flower is an introduced ornamental shrub in the strelitzia family, growing up to 1 m tall with showy flowers and large, long, and wide leaves. The flowers, borne in rigid purplish boatlike bracts, are yellow with dark blue tongue and red stamens. Seedpods resemble green pea pods. Seeds have a tuft of orange-colored hairs attached. The plant is introduced from South Africa and is suitable for warm climates or for growing in homes and greenhouses.

TOXIC PARTS: Seeds and pods.

POISONING: The poisonous principle is an unknown irritant. Ingestion of seeds or pods can cause severe stomach and intestinal distress.

COMMENT: This plant is distinct from the bird-of-paradise bush *(Poinciana gilliesii).*

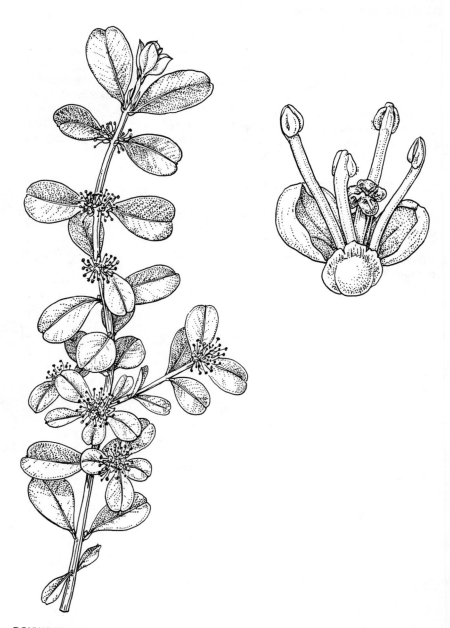

BOXWOOD *(Buxus microphylla)* The unusual flower (enlarged, right) and the attractive dark green leathery leaves are characteristic of this popular shrub.

BOXWOODS

Boxwood

box, boxtree *(Buxus microphylla* and *sempervirens)* and other species

DESCRIPTION AND DISTRIBUTION: Boxwoods are evergreen shrubs or small trees in the box family with angular or winged stems, and small, opposite, entire, oval leaves. The leaves are conspicuously stiff and leathery and dark green. Flowers are in small axillary clusters; fruit is a capsule. They are introduced plants grown extensively throughout the United States as ornamental and hedge plants.

TOXIC PARTS: Leaves and twigs.

POISONING: Leaves and twigs of some boxwoods contain the alkaloid buxine and some other active compounds. However, the plants have a disagreeable odor and bitter taste which cause most animals to avoid them. The leaves of boxwoods are suspected of causing dermatitis.

SYMPTOMS: Nausea, vomiting, stomach pains, and diarrhea, sometimes with bloody feces. If eaten in large quantities, convulsions and death may occur through respiratory failure.

COMMENT: Since these plants have a disagreeable odor and taste, consumption of amounts sufficient to cause death in humans is unlikely.

TEXAS BUCKEYE   The large palmately divided leaves, showy flowers, young fruit (lower right), conspicuous seed capsules (upper right), and shiny dark brown seeds (enlarged, right center) characterize this unusual shrub or small tree.

BUCKEYES, HORSECHESTNUTS

Texas Buckeye
(Aesculus arguta) and other species

DESCRIPTION AND DISTRIBUTION: Texas buckeye is a shrub or small tree in the horsechestnut family. The deciduous leaves are palmately divided into 7 to 9 long pointed leaflets, toothed on the margins. The yellow flowers are borne in showy clusters at the tips of branches. The fruit is a 2- to 3-valved capsule with a thick, leathery, sometimes prickly husk, enclosing one or two brown shiny seeds. Texas buckeye grows on limestone and granitic soils of west Texas, north to Oklahoma and Missouri.

TOXIC PARTS: Seeds, flowers, and leaves.

POISONING: The leaves, flowers, young sprouts, and seeds contain the glycosidic saponin aesculin. Children have been poisoned by eating the seeds or making tea from the leaves and twigs. Honey made from buckeye may also cause poisoning.

SYMPTOMS: Inflammation of mucous membranes, nervous twitching of muscles, weakness, lack of coordination, dilated pupils, nausea, vomiting, diarrhea, depression, paralysis, and stupor.

COMMENTS: Roots, branches, and fruits have been used to stupefy fish in ponds. Roasted seeds have been used for food by Indians. The related, introduced horsechestnut *(Aesculus hippocastanum)* is also poisonous, especially the seeds.

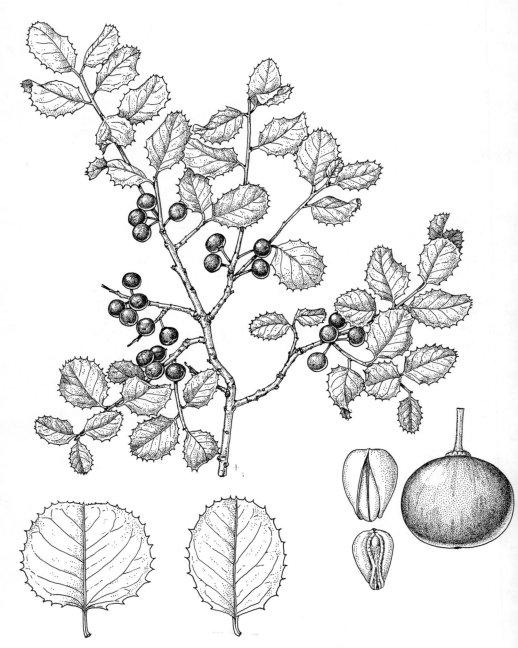

HOLLYLEAF or REDBERRY BUCKTHORN *(Rhamnus crocea)* The hollylike leaves, red berries, and seeds (enlarged, lower right) characterize this attractive shrub.

Buckthorns

coffeeberries, pigeonberries *(Rhamnus sp.)*

DESCRIPTION AND DISTRIBUTION: Buckthorns are native and introduced shrubs or small trees in the buckthorn family with simple leaves
and fleshy fruits. Most species grow in the northwestern and eastern
United States, but several are southwestern species. Many have been
used as ornamentals.

TOXIC PARTS: Bark, leaves, and berries.

POISONING: Buckthorns contain glycosides that are strong laxatives.
An example is cascara, obtained from the bark of *Rhamnus purshiana,*
a Pacific coast species. Poisoning from eating the juicy berry-like fruits
and leaves has been reported from Europe.

SYMPTOMS: Mild to severe cramps and diarrhea.

COMMENTS: Southwestern species have not been reported as poisonous but are suspect because of related toxic species. Plants are seldom
eaten in harmful amounts because of their bitter taste; however, berries
of some species are very attractive, and are eaten. Some species yield
dyes of economic value.

BUTTERCUP Colorful, usually yellow, flowers and large basal leaves are characteristic of this herb.

Buttercups

(Ranunculus sp.)

DESCRIPTION AND DISTRIBUTION: Buttercups are annual or perennial herbs in the buttercup or crowfoot family growing in woods,
meadows, and along streams throughout the temperate and cold countries of the world. Leaves are alternate, entire-to-compound, and largely
basal. Flowers are mostly yellow, borne singly or in clusters at the ends
of seed stalks. Fruits are small, dry one-seeded pods clustered in a
group.

TOXIC PARTS: Entire plant.

POISONING: The seeds and young plants contain the irritant alkaloid
protoanemonin that can severely injure the digestive system and ulcer-
ate the skin. Plants are most toxic in the flowering stage and may be
fatal if eaten in large quantities.

SYMPTOMS: Burning sensation of the mouth and skin, prickling sensation on the skin, nervousness, nausea, vomiting, low blood pressure,
weak pulse, depression, and convulsions.

COMMENTS: These plants are rarely eaten by man and become harmless when dried, so poisoning of humans is unlikely. The leaves and
sap may cause dermatitis in susceptible persons. Cows poisoned by
buttercup produce bitter milk or milk with a reddish color.

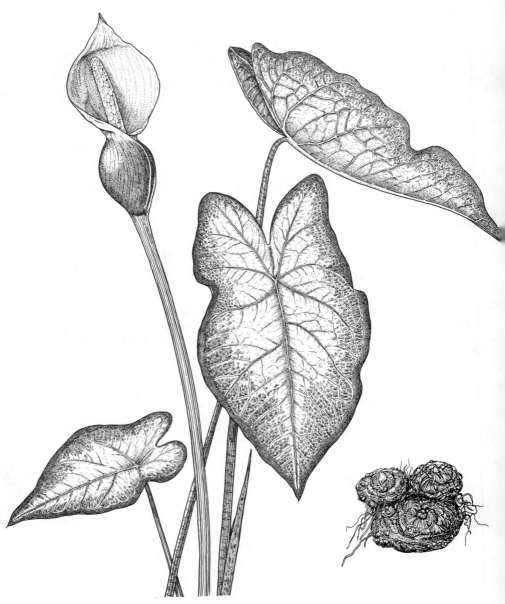

CALADIUM The large, heart-shaped, varicolored leaves, the flowers enclosed in a tubular bract (upper left), and the dormant tuber (lower right) characterize this ornamental plant.

Caladium

(Caladium bicolor) and other species

DESCRIPTION AND DISTRIBUTION: Caladium is an introduced ornamental herb in the arum family. It is stemless and has large varicolored heart-shaped leaves and tuberous roots. Native to tropical America, it is cultivated as a garden plant in the warmer regions and as a house plant in the colder regions. Male and female flowers are borne separately in colorful tubular bracts.

TOXIC PARTS: All parts, especially the leaves and tubers.

POISONING: Caladium contains calcium oxalate crystals and other unidentified principles which cause intense burning, swelling, and paralysis of the tissues when chewed or eaten raw. The intense burning is probably due in part to mechanical injury caused by the sharp crystals and in part to chemical irritation.

SYMPTOMS: Severe burning of the mouth and throat, swelling of the tongue and throat, choking, nausea, vomiting, diarrhea, and salivation. Death may result if tissues about the back of the tongue swell enough to block breathing.

COMMENTS: Symptoms may last for several days or a week or more. Cases of severe poisoning from these plants have not been reported in the United States. The leaves and tubers, when cooked, are eaten as vegetables in tropical America. The powdered leaves are used as an insecticide in the Philippines.

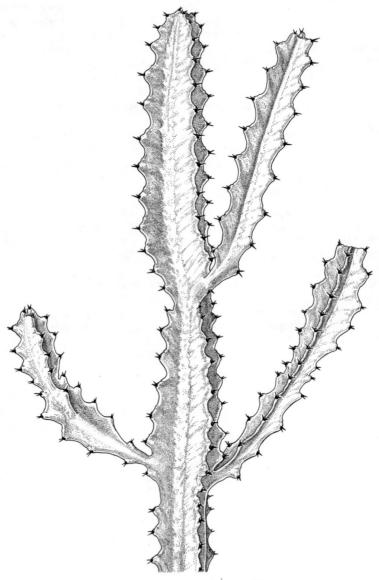

CANDELABRA-CACTUS   Note the distinctive, angled, and spiny succulent stems of this rarely flowering, usually leafless shrub or tree.

Candelabra-Cactus
(Euphorbia lactea)

DESCRIPTION AND DISTRIBUTION: Candelabra-cactus is a many-branched succulent spiny shrub or tree with milky sap. It is a member of the spurge family introduced from the East Indies. Branches are 3- to 4-angled, with a white band down the middle of each side. Ridges are winglike and spiny. The round minute leaves are borne between the spines and fall early. Flowers and fruits are rarely produced in the United States. Spines occur in pairs and are painful to touch. It is widely cultivated as an ornamental in the warmer regions of the United States and as a potted plant in the cooler regions.

TOXIC PARTS: Leaves, stems, and milky sap.

POISONING: This plant is highly toxic and is reported to cause severe stomach upset if the sap is swallowed or the plant eaten. In contact with the skin, the sap produces severe blistering of the skin, temporary blindness and severe dermatitis in susceptible persons.

SYMPTOMS: Severe irritation of the mouth, throat, and skin; temporary blindness, vomiting, diarrhea, and stomach pain.

COMMENTS: This plant should be kept out of reach of children. There are several species similar in appearance, one of which is cowshorn *(Euphorbia grandicornis).* They also have 3-angled winglike stems, are poisonous, and should be regarded with caution.

Cashew Nut
(Anacardium occidentale)

Cashew nut is a tree in the cashew family. The fruit of cashew nut contains a caustic oil, cardol, which will blister the skin on contact. Cardol is removed by a heat process before the nuts are cracked and the wholesome kernels freed for eating. The oil is used as an insect repellent, in making plastics and heavy-duty varnishes, and as a protective coating for machinery. Also, a gum from the tree and an acid (anacardic) within the layers of the nut shell can be caustic.

CASTORBEAN Note the large digitately lobed leaves, the clusters of male flowers (above) and female flowers (below) on the seed stalk, and the spiny seed pod and mottled seed (enlarged, lower right) of this dangerous plant.

Castorbean

castor-oil plant, palma cristi *(Ricinus communis)*

DESCRIPTION AND DISTRIBUTION: Castorbean is generally classed as a shrub but acts as an annual in colder climates. It is a member of the spurge family and grows up to 5 m in height. It has large palmately-lobed leaves. The mottled black, brown, and white glossy seeds are enclosed in a spiny husk and grow in clusters on the seed stalk. Castorbean is cultivated as an ornamental or oil-seed crop mainly in the southern part of the United States and in Hawaii.

TOXIC PARTS: Entire plant, especially the seeds.

POISONING: The seeds, pressed cake, and to a lesser extent the foliage (but not the oil) are extremely toxic when eaten. The poisonous principle is ricin, a phytotoxin. One to 3 seeds can be fatal to a child, 2 to 8 to an adult. Handling or swallowing the seeds may induce bronchial asthma and dermatitis, and the flowers may cause respiratory problems in sensitive individuals.

SYMPTOMS: Burning of the mouth and throat, nausea, vomiting, severe stomach pains, bloody diarrhea, excessive thirst, prostration, dullness of vision, convulsions, kidney failure, and death in 1 to 12 days after eating due to circulatory collapse.

COMMENTS: Removing the immature seeds from ornamental plants is a good precaution. Castorbeans made into necklaces are another potential danger that should be removed. Commercially, the oil is extracted from the seed and used as a medicinal drug, for making soap, and as a lubricant. In the extraction process the poisonous ricin is removed from the oil but remains in the pressed cake. The cake must then be heat-treated to inactivate the phytotoxin so it can be used for cattle feed, but the heat does not remove the allergen.

NIGHT-BLOOMING CESTRUM   The attractive lance-shaped leaves, the fragrant green-ish-white to cream-colored tubular flowers, the clusters of white berries (lower left), and the enlarged berry and seed (left center) characterize this tropical plant.

Cestrums

jessamines *(Cestrum* sp.*)*

DESCRIPTION AND DISTRIBUTION: The cestrums are shrubs or small trees of the nightshade family introduced from tropical America. Leaves are alternate, simple, narrow, and entire. The fragrant and showy red, yellow, white, or greenish tubular flowers are borne in terminal or axillary clusters. The fruit is a small white-to-purple berry. Cestrums have escaped in the Southeast and are grown in the Southwest as ornamentals.

TOXIC PARTS: Berries and leaves.

POISONING: Eating any part of these plants can result in symptoms resembling atropine poisoning. Fruits are the most toxic part and children and pets have been poisoned by eating the berries. The leaves are also high in saponins.

SYMPTOMS: Nausea, vomiting, salivation, headache, fever, pupil dilation, dizziness, hallucinations, nervousness, muscular spasms, elevated temperature, and paralysis. Also, difficulty in breathing, depression, uneasiness, throat irritation, and sneezing may occur.

COMMENTS: Cases of human poisoning by day cestrum *(Cestrum diurnum)* have been reported in this country. The heavy perfume of nightblooming jessamine *(Cestrum nocturnum)* is reported to have a narcotic effect and has caused headaches, nausea, and dizziness. However, patients responded to treatment and recovery was complete.

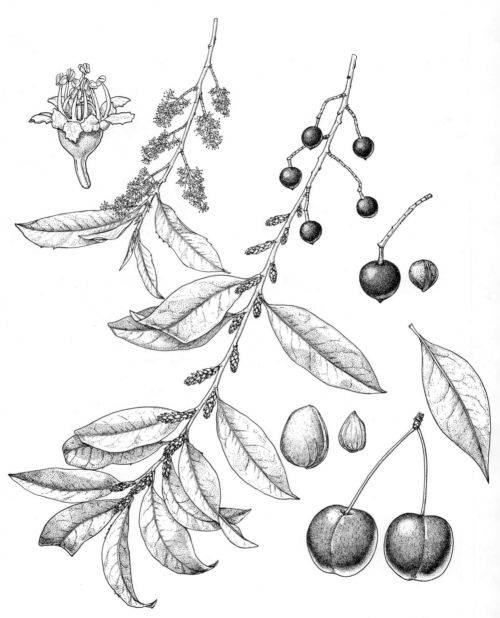

CHERRIES   At upper left are the flowering and fruiting branches, fruits, and seed of the more toxic laurel cherry; at lower right are the leaf, fruits, seed and kernel of the sweet cherry.

CHERRIES

Sour Cherry
(Prunus cerasus)

Sweet Cherry
(Prunus avium)

Laurel Cherry
Carolina cherry *(Prunus caroliniana)*

DESCRIPTION AND DISTRIBUTION: Sour cherry is a small deciduous tree with oval, doubly toothed leaves, white to pink flowers, and small, round, sour, bright-red fruits. Sweet cherry is a large deciduous tree with smooth bark, large oblong doubly toothed clustered leaves, white to pink flowers, and round-to-oblong, pink to dark-red fruits. Both are cultivated fruits introduced from Eurasia and grown in temperate regions.

The laurel cherry is a small evergreen tree native to the central and eastern United States that is widely planted in the Southwest as an ornamental. Leaves are lance-shaped, sharp-pointed, and more or less smooth-margined. Flowers are white and borne in clusters on the stem; the fruits are small, black, and rounded with a point on the end.

TOXIC PARTS: Seeds, leaves, and bark

POISONING: The seeds and leaves of cherries contain the cyanogenic glycoside amygdalin which breaks down into the toxic hydrocyanic (prussic) acid when hydrolyzed. The seeds are the most toxic, but children can also be poisoned by chewing on twigs or making tea from the leaves. The leaves are most dangerous early in the season.

SYMPTOMS: Dizziness, spasms, stupor, twitching, paralysis of vocal cords, convulsions, and coma. In mild cases, symptoms may include weakness, incoordination, difficulty in breathing, headache, nausea, vomiting, and irregular heartbeat. In severe cases, death may result.

COMMENTS: The fleshy parts of the sweet and sour cherries are edible, but those of the laurel cherry are not. The laurel cherry is more dangerous than the edible ones. Since cherry pits and leaves are not normally eaten by man the danger of human poisoning is low. In medicine, powdered laurel cherry leaves are used to relax muscles and control coughing.

43

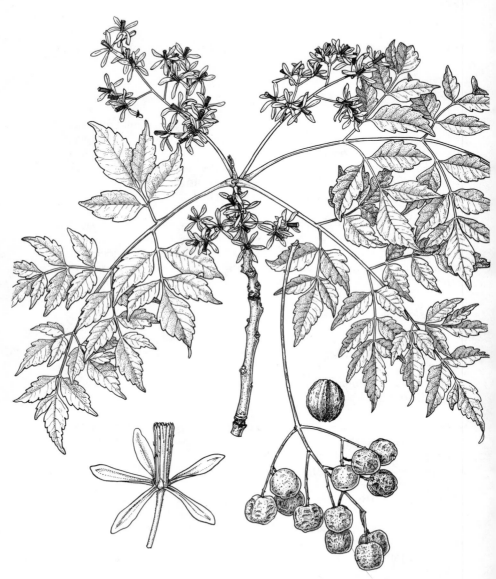

CHINABERRY Note the unique flowers (enlarged, lower left), the pinnately compound leaves, the wrinkled berries, and seed (enlarged, lower right) of this popular shade tree.

Chinaberry

China tree, Chinaball tree, umbrella tree *(Melia azedarach)*

DESCRIPTION AND DISTRIBUTION: Chinaberry is a small introduced deciduous tree in the mahogany family, with twice pinnately divided leaves and toothed or lobed leaflets. The purple flowers and the yellow, wrinkled, rounded berries (drupes) are borne in terminal clusters. It has been introduced in the warmer southern part of the United States and in Hawaii as a shade and ornamental tree.

TOXIC PARTS: Berries, bark, flowers, and leaves.

POISONING: Most poisonings result from eating the pulp of the fruits. The toxic principle is a resinoid (or alkaloid) which causes narcotic effects. The toxin is contained mainly in the pulp of the fruits and in the bark and flowers.

SYMPTOMS: Nausea, vomiting, diarrhea, narcotic effects, irregular breathing, and respiratory distress. Occasionally death may result from suffocation caused by paralysis.

COMMENTS: Most human poisonings occur in children, for 6 to 8 berries can cause death. Rural people, when drying peaches in the sun, scatter chinaberries among the fruits to repel insects and worms. The berries have also been used to make insecticide and flea powder; and the bark, to stupefy fish. The relatively harmless seeds are used to make necklaces.

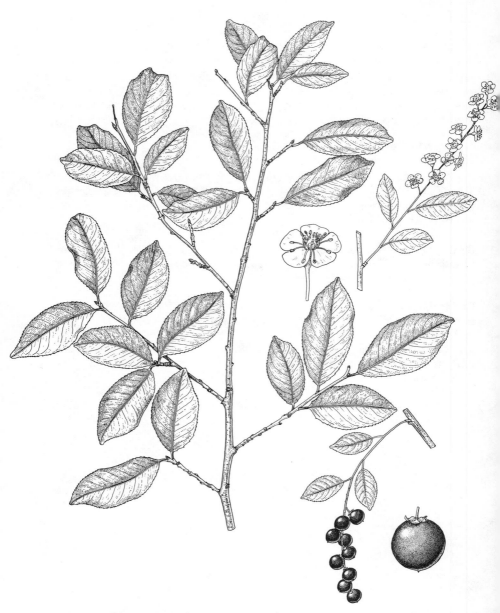

SOUTHWESTERN CHOKECHERRY   Oval leaves with saw-toothed edges, white flowers (upper right), and clusters of black cherries (lower right) are characteristic of this attractive native shrub.

CHOKECHERRIES

Southwestern Chokecherry
(Prunus serotina var. *virens)*

Western Chokecherry
(Prunus virginiana var. *demissa)*

Black Western Chokecherry
(Prunus virginiana var. *melanocarpa)*

DESCRIPTION AND DISTRIBUTION: Chokecherries are native and range in size from small trees to large shrubs. A member of the rose family, the plant has oval, finely toothed leaves. The bark is smooth on young twigs, becoming rough and scaly on older stems. The white to pink flowers and fruit are in elongated clusters. The fruit is a red or black cherry with a hard bony seed. Plants grow along streams and in forests in the West and Southwest as the common names indicate.

TOXIC PARTS: All parts, but particularly bark, leaves, and seeds.

POISONING: The bark, leaves, and seeds contain the cyanogenic glycoside amygdalin which breaks down into hydrocyanic (prussic) acid when hydrolized by freezing or partial wilting. Children have been poisoned by eating the seeds, making tea from the leaves, or chewing on leaves. Symptoms of poisoning can occur suddenly.

SYMPTOMS: Difficulty in breathing, paralysis of the voice, twitching, spasms, stupor, coma, and death. In mild cases, symptoms may include nausea, vomiting, headache, muscular weakness, and irregular heartbeat.

COMMENTS: The fruit is edible if the seeds are discarded. Leaves are most toxic in the spring, on new shoots, and when partially wilted. The bark and dried fruit are sometimes used as a source of medicine.

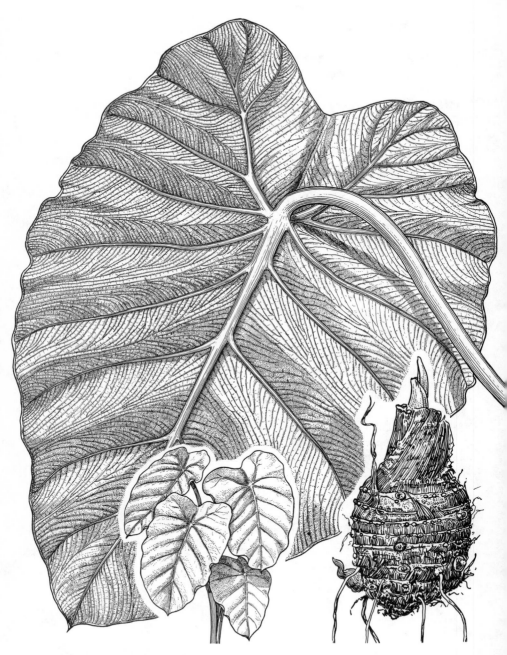

ELEPHANT'S-EAR Note the large leaf, shaped like an elephant's ear, and the scaly
tuber of this large ornamental plant.

Clematis

virgin's-bower *(Clematis sp.)*

Clematis species are native or cultivated, perennial herbs or climbing woody vines found in the North Temperate Zone. They are members of the poisonous crowfoot or buttercup family which contain alkaloids that can cause stomach upset, nervous symptoms, depression, and even death. Therefore they should be treated with caution. The leaves can also cause dermatitis in susceptible individuals.

COLOCASIAS

Elephant's-Ear
(Colocasia antiquorum)

Taro, Dasheen
(Colocasia esculenta)

DESCRIPTION AND DISTRIBUTION: These plants are introduced herbs in the arum family, grown as ornamentals and for their edible tubers. Leaves are large, varicolored, and heart-shaped, up to 65 cm long. Flowers are enclosed in a leafy bract. Taro has large edible tubers, but the tubers of elephant's-ear are toxic. The plants are grown indoors as ornamental potted plants in most of the United States and outdoors in subtropical climates. They are occasionally an escape in Florida.

TOXIC PARTS: All parts, except the tubers of taro.

POISONING: The plants contain calcium oxalate crystals and the protein enzyme, asparagine, which cause burning and swelling of the mouth and throat if chewed. Other unknown toxic substances are also present. In severe cases swelling of the mouth and throat can cause death by choking. However, recorded deaths have occurred only in experimental animals.

SYMPTOMS: Severe burning of mucous membranes and swelling of the tongue, mouth, and throat; choking, nausea, vomiting, diarrhea, and salivation.

COMMENTS: The large edible tubers of tara or dasheen are used to make "poi" in Hawaii. A closely related genus, *Alocasia,* also called elephant's-ear, has similar toxic properties and edible tubers.

49

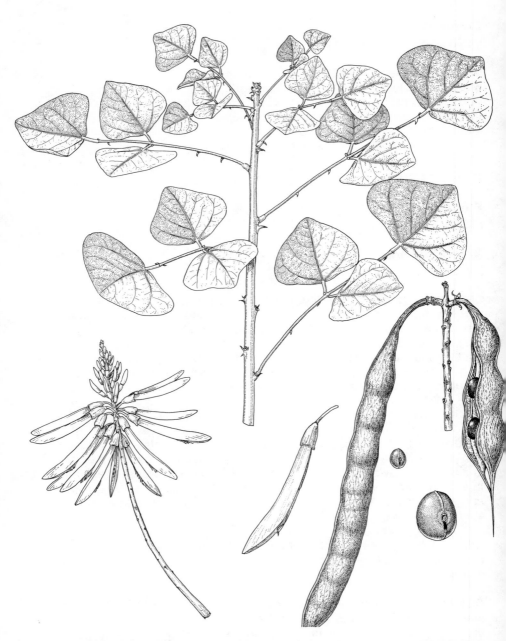

WESTERN CORALBEAN The 3-parted leaves, the spiny stems, the beautiful flaming-red flowers (lower left), and the showy coral-colored beans and rough seed pods (lower right) characterize this interesting plant.

CORALBEANS
coraltrees

Western Coralbean
Indian bean, chilicote *(Erythrina flabelliformis)* and other species

DESCRIPTION AND DISTRIBUTION: Western coralbean is a prickly shrub or small tree with leaves pinnately divided into three large fan-shaped leaflets. The long, showy, bright-red flowers are borne in the axils of the leaves or at the ends of the stem. Seed pods are large and thick containing bright-red seeds. It is native to the southwestern United States and northern Mexico, where it is often planted as an ornamental.

TOXIC PARTS: All parts, especially the raw beans.

POISONING: The beans of western coralbean are believed poisonous although the claims are undocumented. However, they should be considered dangerous since the beans, leaves, and bark of Asian coraltree *(Erythrina variegata)* contain saponins, hydrocyanic acid, and the toxic alkaloid erythrinine, and cause poisoning if chewed raw. Also, in Mexico the beans of another coralbean *(Erythrina herbacea* var. *arborea)* contain numerous toxic alkaloids and are used as a rat poison. However, the boiled or roasted beans of coraltree are reported to be edible, and the leaves and flowers can be eaten when cooked as a vegetable.

SYMPTOMS: The alkaloid erythrinine acts as a depressant on the central nervous system, and one seed can cause illness in an adult.

COMMENTS: The bark of coraltree acts as an astringent and is used to reduce fever, relieve dysentery, and reduce eye inflammation; the beans are used internally and externally to treat cancer. In the Southwest, the showy flowers and beautiful leaves of western coralbean make it an attractive ornamental. The bright red beans are used to make necklaces and other ornaments.

TEXAS CROTON *(Croton texensis)*   Note the simple entire leaf; the flowers (enlarged, right center) male, above, and female, below; and the seed and seed pod (enlarged, lower left). The entire plant is covered with gray star-shaped hairs (enlarged, lower right).

Crotons
(Croton sp.)

DESCRIPTION AND DISTRIBUTION: Native crotons are annual or perennial herbs or shrubs belonging to the spurge family. The plants have a strong characteristic odor. Leaves are simple, often with star-shaped hairs and/or glands. The male and female flowers are borne in separate flowers, sometimes on separate plants. The seeds are borne in capsules. The plant is common in the Southwest.

TOXIC PART: Oil of croton contained in the seeds.

POISONING: The Hopi Indians and pioneers used croton as a laxative. The oil of croton from the Asiatic species *(Croton tiglium)* is such a powerful cathartic that a few drops can kill a dog. Cattle die from eating hay containing native plants of croton, but the live plants are so unpalatable that they are rarely ingested in sufficient quantity to cause serious poisoning. The toxic principle in native plants is also believed to be oil of croton. Misuse of these plants or oil of croton as a medicine can cause poisoning in humans.

SYMPTOMS: Burning pain in the mouth and stomach, rapid heartbeat, bloody diarrhea, and coma. In severe cases death may result.

COMMENTS: The Hopi Indians also used croton as an eyewash. Because of the unpalatable nature of these plants, consumption of enough of the plants to cause death is unlikely.

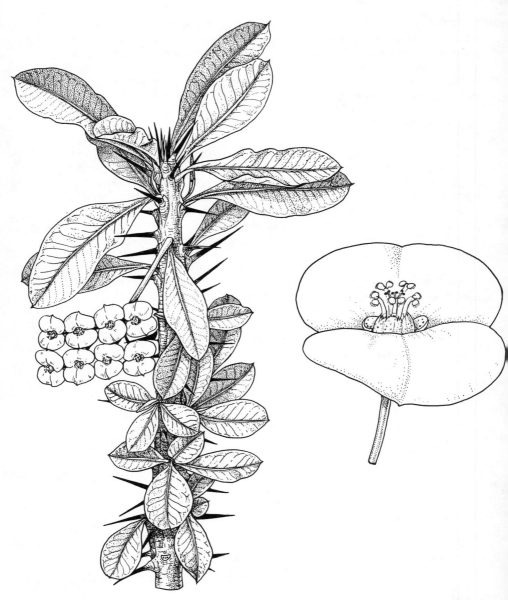

CROWN-OF-THORNS The spiny, usually leafless stems and charming flower clusters characterize this unusual plant.

Crown-of-Thorns

Christ-thorn *(Euphorbia milii,* formerly *Euphorbia splendens)*

DESCRIPTION AND DISTRIBUTION: Crown-of-thorns is a cultivated house or patio shrub in the spurge family. Introduced from Madagascar, it can be planted outside in the warmer areas of the United States. It is a spiny branched plant which reaches 1.5 m in height and has milky juice. The lance-shaped leaves occur mostly on young growth. The flowers are subtended with two broad, red or yellow showy bracts that make it a very attractive plant. Fruit is a 3-lobed capsule.

TOXIC PARTS: Entire plant.

POISONING: Contact with the milky sap causes a dermatitis with the symptoms of blisters and inflammation in humans. If eaten, the plant causes severe digestive upset.

SYMPTOMS: Severe irritation to the mouth, throat, and stomach; abdominal pain, fainting, vomiting, and diarrhea.

COMMENTS: These plants are less potent than wild spurges but their use as ornamentals makes them more readily available to curious children. The caustic sap has been used as an astringent to check the flow of blood.

DAFFODIL Note the large showy flower with a fringed corona (tube) growing singly on leafless flower stalks, the scaly bulb (lower right), and the seed (enlarged) and seed pod (lower left) of this colorful herb.

Daffodil

trumpet narcissus *(Narcissus pseudonarcissus)*

DESCRIPTION AND DISTRIBUTION: Daffodil is an early-spring-flow-ering bulbous forb of the amaryllis family, introduced from Europe. Leaves are basal, long, and narrow. Showy yellow flowers are large and tubular, growing singly on the ends of the flower stalks. Fruit is a lobed capsule. Plants are grown indoors as house plants or outdoors in gardens.

TOXIC PART: Bulbs.

POISONING: This popular spring-flowering plant may cause diges-tive upset even when eaten in small quantities. The bulb is the most dangerous.

SYMPTOMS: Nausea, vomiting, diarrhea, trembling, convulsions, and possible death if eaten in quantity.

COMMENTS: Since small amounts cause vomiting and ejection of toxic parts, death from eating these plants is rare. Leaves and bulbs may also cause dermatitis to susceptible persons.

SACRED DATURA Note the long trumpet-shaped flowers, the large leaves, and the spiny nodding fruit and enlarged seed (lower right) of this dangerous plant.

DATURAS

Sacred Datura
Indianapple, tolguacha, moonflower *(Datura meteloides)*

Jimsonweed
Thornapple, Jamestown-weed, stinkweed, datura *(Datura stramonium)*

DESCRIPTION AND DISTRIBUTION: Daturas are coarse weedy herbs in the nightshade family with stout stems and foul-smelling herbage. Leaves are large and oval with wavy margins. The fragrant flowers are large, tubular and showy, varying in color from white to purple. The fruit is a round, nodding or erect, prickly capsule. Sacred datura is a perennial common throughout the Southwest; jimsonweed is an annual naturalized throughout the United States.

TOXIC PARTS: All parts, particularly the seeds and leaves.

POISONING: Toxicity results from the alkaloids hyoscyamine, atropine, and scopolamine. People have been poisoned from sucking nectar, eating the seeds and unripened seed pods, and drinking tea made from the leaves. Twenty seeds are sufficient to cause poisoning in an adult. Plants are frequently ingested for their hallucinogenic effects; contact with the plant may cause dermatitis in susceptible persons.

SYMPTOMS: Dry mouth, thirst, redness of skin, disturbed vision, pupil dilation, nausea, vomiting, headache, hallucination, excitement, rapid pulse, delirium, incoherent speech, apparent insanity, convulsions, elevated temperature, high blood pressure, and coma. In severe cases death may result.

COMMENTS: Indians administered the seeds to prevent miscarriage. In modern medicine, atropine and related alkaloids are used to treat eye, skin, rectal, stomach, and intestinal disorders. Personal use of the plants for treatment of asthma or as a hallucinogen can be dangerous. Even sleeping near the fragrant flowers can cause headache, nausea, dizziness, and weakness. Children using the flowers for play trumpets have been poisoned.

FOOTHILL DEATHCAMAS   Note the long slender leaves, scaly bulb, delicate flowers, 3-celled seed pods. and seed (enlarged, lower right) of this deadly plant.

DEATHCAMASES

Foothill Deathcamas
(Zigadenus paniculatus) and other species

DESCRIPTION AND DISTRIBUTION: Deathcamases are perennial bulbous forbs of the lily family. They resemble wild onions in appearance but the onion odor is lacking. Leaves are long and slender with parallel veins. The pale yellow to pink flowers occur in clusters on slender seedstalks. The fruit is a 3-celled capsule. Various species occur throughout the United States but are most abundant in the West.

TOXIC PARTS: Entire plant, especially the bulb.

POISONING: The toxins are the alkaloids zygadenine, veratrine, and others. Humans, especially children, have been poisoned by eating the bulbs and the flowers. All species are considered dangerous.

SYMPTOMS: Excessive watering of the mouth, muscular weakness, slow heartbeat, low blood pressure, subnormal temperature, nausea, vomiting, diarrhea, stomach pains, prostration, coma, and occasionally death.

COMMENTS: Flour made from the bulbs of deathcamas produced violent intestinal symptoms in the expeditionary forces of Lewis and Clark. Later, pioneers were killed by eating the bulbs which were mistaken for the edible camas and wild onion or garlic.

DOGBANE Note the paired, entire, variable-shaped leaves, the clusters of small flowers (enlarged, right), and the slender pods and tufted seeds (far right) of this milky-juiced herb.

DOGBANES

Dogbane
Indian-hemp *(Apocynum cannabinum)* and other species

DESCRIPTION AND DISTRIBUTION: Dogbanes are perennial herbs in the dogbane family with milky juice and somewhat woody stems that grow from creeping rootstocks. Leaves are simple, smooth, and oppositely-paired. The bell-shaped, small, white to pink flowers are borne in clusters at the ends of the axillary stems. The long, slender, round, paired seedpods are filled with seeds, each with a tuft of long white hairs. Various species are found throughout North America growing in fields and forests and along streams and roadsides.

TOXIC PARTS: Entire plant.

POISONING: Poisoning of humans has not been reported in this country, but the plant should be suspect since it contains the toxic glycoside cymarin, resins, and other toxic substances poisonous to cats, dogs, and other animals. It should be noted that some of the data reported in the literature is unreliable, having been drawn from a report confusing oleander with dogbane.

SYMPTOMS: Symptoms in animals include increased temperature and pulse, coldness of extremities, dilation of pupils of the eyes, discoloration of mouth and nostrils, sore mouth, sweating, loss of appetite, upset stomach, and death.

COMMENTS: Compounds from the root of dogbane have been used in medicine as a heart stimulant. Indians used the bark to make cordage, hence the name Indian-hemp. This common name is also applied to marihuana.

DUMBCANE   Note the large variegated leaves of this attractive ornamental. Flowers and fruits are rarely produced.

Dumbcanes

(Dieffenbachia sp.)

DESCRIPTION AND DISTRIBUTION: Dumbcanes are tall shrubby plants in the arum family which reach 2 m in height. The leaves are large, oblong, and entirely green or mottled white and green. Male and female flowers are produced separately in folded leaflike bracts. Plants have a skunklike odor when bruised. Introduced from tropical America they are common ornamental plants grown in houses, offices, and businesses throughout the United States and outdoors in the subtropical parts of the country.

TOXIC PARTS: Entire plants, especially the stems.

POISONING: If eaten or chewed, severe burning and swelling occurs in the throat and mouth caused by needlelike calcium oxalate crystals and an enzyme, possibly asparagine. Swelling of the mouth, tongue, and throat may interfere with speech, swallowing, and breathing for a week or more. In severe cases swelling of the mouth and tongue can cause death by choking. Deaths have occurred in experimental animals but have not been reported in humans.

SYMPTOMS: Severe burning and swelling of mucous membranes of the mouth and throat, choking, nausea, vomiting, diarrhea, and copious salivation.

COMMENTS: Another member of the arum family, jack-in-the-pulpit *(Arisaema triphyllum),* native to northeastern United States and southern Canada, can cause similar injury to the mouth if the roots are eaten in quantity. Handling the plant or contact with the white milky juice of dumbcane may cause dermatitis in susceptible individuals.

EGGPLANT Large wavy-margined leaves, violet-purple flowers, large oval fruits, and kidney-shaped seed (enlarged, center) are characteristic of this common garden vegetable.

Eggplant
(Solanum melongena)

DESCRIPTION AND DISTRIBUTION: Eggplant is a tall, spiny, bushy, perennial herb or shrub of the nightshade family often cultivated as an annual. Leaves are ovate and have wavy or lobed margins. Flowers are violet-purple and usually solitary in the leaf axils. Fruit is a large, usually purplish-black, glossy, oval-shaped, fleshy berry. Berries of other varieties are white, yellowish, or striped. Introduced from Africa and Asia, eggplant is widely cultivated in the warmer areas of the United States and Mexico.

TOXIC PARTS: Leaves, stems, and fruit may be poisonous.

POISONING: Eggplant contains toxic solanaceous alkaloids, belongs to a poisonous family, and has long had a reputation for toxicity. However, cases of poisoning have not been documented.

SYMPTOMS: None documented.

COMMENT: For safety, eat only cooked, healthy ripe fruits.

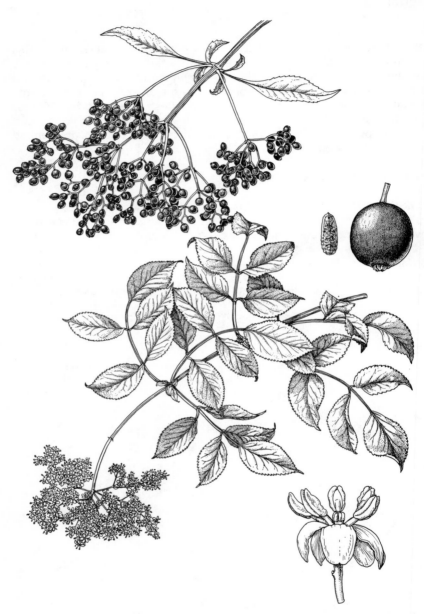

MEXICAN ELDER Note the large pinnately divided leaves and the dense flower and fruit clusters. The enlarged berry and seed are shown in the upper right, the enlarged flower in the lower right.

ELDERBERRIES

Mexican Elder

tapiro *(Sambucus mexicana)* and other species

DESCRIPTION AND DISTRIBUTION: Elderberries are native shrubs or small trees in the honeysuckle family with soft wood and pithy stems. Leaves are large and pinnately divided into 5 to 11 ovate toothed leaflets. Flowers and fruits are in large flat-topped or pyramidal clusters. Flowers are cream colored; berries are black, blue, or red, and juicy. Various species are found throughout the United States in mountains and forests, except the southwestern Mexican elder which grows mainly along stream bottoms at lower elevations.

TOXIC PARTS: Roots, stems, leaves, bark, and unripe berries.

POISONING: Fresh leaves, stems, and roots contain a poisonous alkaloid and the cyanogenic glycoside sambunigrin which may cause cyanide poisoning. Children have been poisoned by the bark when making blowguns and whistles out of the stems. The roots have also caused poisoning in children. Uncooked berries may cause nausea if too many are eaten. The red elderberries are believed to be the most toxic.

SYMPTOMS: Nausea, vomiting, and diarrhea.

COMMENTS: The flowers and ripe fruit are harmless, the berries frequently being used in making pies, wine, jelly, and pancakes. The fruit is relished by birds and other wildlife. The flowers, fruits, and bark have been used in medicine as a cathartic and emetic, and to treat rheumatism, syphilis, dropsy, epilepsy, sores, and tumors.

ERGOT Note the ergot structures extruding from the seed heads of barley (right). These structures replace the normal grain and are the toxic stage in the life cycle of ergot.

Ergots

(Claviceps purpurea) and other species

DESCRIPTION AND DISTRIBUTION: Ergots are fungi that parasitize the grains of several cultivated grains and native grasses. A mat of filaments develops in place of and in the shape of the grain, forming a hard pink or purplish structure (sclerotium) sometimes 3 to 4 times the size of the normal grain. This is the poisonous ergot stage in the life cycle. The sclerotia fall to the soil with the grain, overwinter, then produce a sexual spore stage (ascospore) in the spring which infects the new grass crop.

TOXIC PART: Ergot stage of life cycle.

POISONING: Poisoning in humans occurs when infected, uncleaned grains such as wheat, barley, and rye, or products made from them, are eaten. The toxins are alkaloids, amines, and other nitrogen-containing compounds. Grain containing over 1% sclerotia is considered dangerous for human consumption. Chronic poisoning results from ingestion of small amounts over a period of several weeks to a few months; acute poisoning from larger amounts is usually due to excessive medicinal applications. A lethal dose may be as small as 1 gm of ergot extract.

SYMPTOMS: In chronic ergot poisoning the blood vessels contract and blood flow is restricted, resulting in dry gangrene and death of tissues, especially in the extremities. Symptoms include numbness, tingling, coldness of extremities, pain in the chest, gangrene of the fingers and toes, tremors, and convulsions. Acute poisoning results in muscle and abdominal pain, nausea, vomiting, diarrhea, constriction of the throat, disturbance of speech and vision, delirium, tingling, numbness of extremities, weakness, convulsions, and coma. Acute poisoning may also cause abortion in pregnant women and gangrene in the extremities after several days.

COMMENTS: Human poisoning by ergot was common and much feared in the past, but with modern methods of handling and cleaning grain and federal laws prohibiting selling of grain containing more than 0.3% ergot sclerotia by weight, ergot poisoning from grains in the United States is rare. Medical applications in the treatment of migraine headaches and for childbirth occasionally result in acute poisoning. Lysergic acid is derived from ergot and is the base ingredient used to produce the hallucinogenic drug LSD (lysergic acid diethylamide).

71

GOLDENROD EUPATORIUM *(Eupatorium solidaginifolium)*   This low white-flowered shrub or half-shrub is a common southwestern species. Note the lance-shaped leaves, terminal flower heads, tubular flowers (upper right), and 5-ribbed fruit (achene) with a crown of bristles (lower right).

Eupatoriums

snakeroots, thoroughworts *(Eupatorium sp.)*

DESCRIPTION AND DISTRIBUTION: White snakeroot *(Eupatorium rugosum)*, a herb in the sunflower family, is found in the East and Midwest. It causes milk sickness in humans and was a major cause of death in early colonial times until its cause was discovered. There are many species of *Eupatorium* in the Southwest which may also cause poisonings.

TOXIC PARTS: Entire plant.

POISONING: The entire plant contains the higher alcohol tremetol and certain glycosides which accumulate in the milk of cows feeding on the plants. Humans drinking the raw milk are then poisoned. Recovery from non-lethal illness is slow.

SYMPTOMS: Weakness, nausea, loss of appetite, severe vomiting, tremors, liver damage, labored breathing, jaundice, constipation, weakness, prostration, dizziness, delirium, convulsions, coma, and death. Also, there may be a decrease or loss of urination due to kidney damage.

COMMENTS: With modern milk processing procedures, contaminated milk is diluted and danger of poisoning is low. The only danger is from drinking raw milk from the family cow grazing on the plants. Fresh plants are the most toxic. For some unknown reason poisonings are more common from cows grazing bottomlands and wooded areas.

CALIFORNIA FALSE-HELLEBORE   Note the large parallel-veined clasping leaves, the large clusters of flowers, the 3-lobed seed capsule (enlarged, lower right), and seed (enlarged, lower center) of this conspicuous plant.

FALSE-HELLEBORES

California False-Hellebore
corn lily, skunkcabbage *(Veratrum californicum),* and other species

DESCRIPTION AND DISTRIBUTION: False-hellebores are tall, broad-leaved herbs of the lily family growing up to 2 m in height from a thick rootstock. Leaves are large, alternate, pleated, clasping, and parallel-veined. Flowers are numerous and white to greenish in large terminal clusters. The fruit is a 3-lobed capsule. Various species are found throughout North America in wet meadows, forests, and along streams.

TOXIC PARTS: Entire plant.

POISONING: False-hellebores contain alkaloids, such as veradridene and veratrine, that act on the cardiovascular system, respiration, nerve fibers, and skeletal muscles. Hallucinations have been reported and the plants are suspected of causing dermatitis.

SYMPTOMS: Nausea, vomiting, diarrhea, stomach pains, reduced blood pressure, slow pulse, lowered body temperature, shallow breathing, salivation, unpleasant taste, muscular weakness, nervousness, spasms, convulsions, and general paralysis. Death may result in severe cases.

COMMENTS: The plants have been used for centuries as a source of drugs and as a source of insecticide. The leaves resemble cabbage and are often collected as a natural food with unpleasant results. Consumption of false-hellebore by ewes the first three weeks after pregnancy can cause abortion and a malformation of lambs called monkey face. Similar effects are a possibility in humans, if derivatives of false-hellebore are given as a medicine or for other purposes.

BRACKEN FERN Note the large pinnately divided leaf-like frond, the spore-bearing frond (lower left), fiddleneck (lower center), unfolding fiddleneck (lower right), and the underground rootstock (lower right) of this primitive plant.

FERNS

Bracken Fern
brake fern *(Pteridium aquilinum)* and other species

DESCRIPTION AND DISTRIBUTION: Bracken fern is a tall forb in the fern family, growing up to 1.5 m tall from horizontal rootstocks. Fronds (leaves) are large, somewhat fan-shaped, and pinnately divided several times. Edges of the fronds are rolled under and mature fronds have numerous brown, circular, spore-bearing bodies on the underside. It grows worldwide in mountains and forests.

TOXIC PARTS: Entire plant, especially the rootstocks.

POISONING: Plants contain the enzyme thiaminase which causes a thiamine (Vitamin B_1) deficiency in the diet of animals when the raw plants make up 20% or more of the diet over a period of about a month. In some areas, it is popular for humans to eat the young fern fiddlenecks (unexpanded fronds) in salads or as a hot vegetable. Since heat destroys the enzyme thiaminase, the cooked fronds would present no problem. Also, since animals and presumably humans, would have to eat a high percentage of raw ferns in the diet for a long period of time, the danger of human poisoning would be limited to unusual circumstances.

SYMPTOMS: Symptoms in animals include loss of weight, mucous discharge from nostrils and mouth, listlessness, incoordination, muscle tremors, elevated temperature, bloody feces, convulsions, and collapse. Bracken fern can be fatal to animals in several days to several weeks, but human deaths have not been recorded.

COMMENTS: The probability of human poisoning by bracken fern is extremely remote. However, mistaking young plants of the deadly poison-hemlock or water-hemlock for edible fern fiddlenecks could be disastrous.

FOUR-O'CLOCK Note the lance-shaped leaves, the trumpet-shaped flowers, the large tuberous root, and the ribbed seed (lower center and right) of this unusual plant.

FOUR-O'CLOCKS

Four-O'Clock

marvel-of-Peru, beauty-of-the-night *(Mirabilis jalapa),* and other species

DESCRIPTION AND DISTRIBUTION: Four-o'clock is a tuberous, erect, many-branched perennial or annual (depending on climate) forb in the four-o'clock family which reaches 1 m in height. Leaves occur in pairs and are deep green, ovate, and pointed. Flowers are tubular and red, pink, yellow, or white, often striped and mottled. Introduced from tropical America, it is a popular ornamental in old-fashioned gardens and has often escaped in the Southwest and warmer regions of the United States.

TOXIC PARTS: Roots and seeds.

POISONING: The plants contain the alkaloid trigonelline which has caused poisoning in children.

SYMPTOMS: Acute stomach pain, nausea, vomiting, diarrhea, and irritation of the skin and mucous membranes.

COMMENT: Children normally recover without serious complications.

WRIGHT GROUNDCHERRY *(Physalis wrightii)*   The wavy-margined leaves, colorful flowers with flared openings, inflated seed pod (lower far left), and seed (enlarged, lower near left) characterize this southwestern forb.

Groundcherries

Chinese lanterns, husktomatoes *(Physalis sp.)*

DESCRIPTION AND DISTRIBUTION: Groundcherries are both native and introduced, erect or decumbent, annual or perennial herbs in the nightshade family. Leaves are simple, alternate, petioled, and toothed. Flowers are solitary in leaf axils and may be white, yellow, or purple. Fruits are round berries that vary from yellow to red to purple. The fruits are enclosed in a lantern-shaped loose-fitting pod. Both native and introduced species are widely grown in the United States for their fruits and as ornamentals.

TOXIC PARTS: Unripe fruit and leaves.

POISONING: The unripe fruit and leaves of some species have caused poisoning.

SYMPTOMS: None recorded. Probably no more serious than an upset stomach.

COMMENT: The mature fruits are prized for making jams, jellies, and pies.

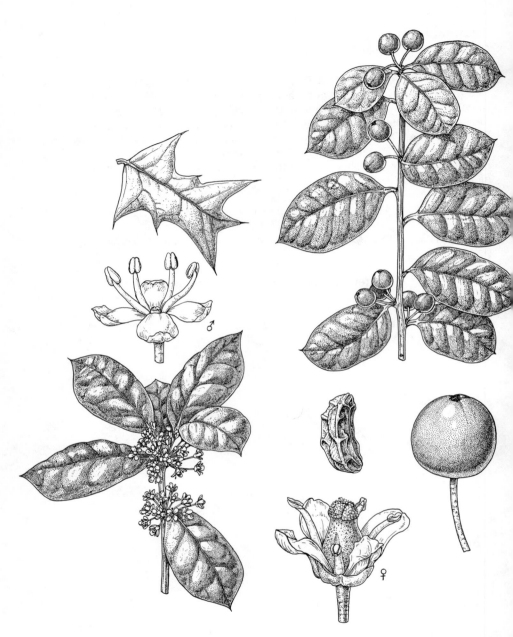

HOLLY   **Note** the smooth to spiny variation in leaves (depending on species), the clusters of **flowers** and fruits in the leaf axils, the male flowers (enlarged, left center) and female flowers (enlarged, lower center), and the berry and seed (enlarged, lower right) of these attractive Christmas plants.

Hollies
(Ilex sp.)

DESCRIPTION AND DISTRIBUTION: Hollies are native and intro-duced, deciduous and evergreen shrubs and trees in the holly family. Leaves are leathery, shiny, and usually toothed or spiny. Flowers are white to greenish, borne singly or in clusters. Fruits are round and berry-like, red or black. Evergreen hollies are cultivated in the warm moist southern climates of the United States; deciduous ones are in the north-ern climates.

TOXIC PARTS: Berries.

POISONING: The berries of all species are reported to be poisonous if eaten in quantity. The toxic principle is ilicin. Although not considered very poisonous, the attractive red or black berries should be considered dangerous to small children.

SYMPTOMS: Nausea, vomiting, diarrhea, and stupor due to depression of the central nervous system.

COMMENTS: These are the hollies used extensively as Christmas decorations. Indians and early settlers used the leaves to make a mild brew such as "youpon tea."

HOPBUSH   Note the long and narrow, often sticky leaves, the male flowering branch and enlarged flower (upper left), the female flowering branch and enlarged flower (upper right), the developing fruit (lower right), and the fruiting branch (lower center).

Hopbush

(Dodonaea viscosa var. *angustifolia)*

DESCRIPTION AND DISTRIBUTION: Hopbush is a shrub or small tree in the soapberry family. Leaves are dark green, alternate, entire, long, narrow, and sticky. The yellowish green flowers are borne in clusters; sexes are in separate flowers. Fruits are dry and 3-winged (hoplike). Native to the Southwest, hopbush grows in canyons and dry rocky slopes of the upper desert and desert grassland.

TOXIC PARTS: Leaves and bark.

POISONING: Various medicinal preparations have been made from the leaves and bark. The plant also contains saponins that are poisonous, and it has been used as a fish poison. Therefore, use of the plant for medicinal purposes by the amateur could be dangerous, but under ordinary circumstances it is unlikely that hopbush would cause serious poisoning in humans.

SYMPTOMS: None reported.

COMMENTS: Its fruits have been used as a substitute for hops. Also, its winged fruits and shiny green leaves make it attractive as an ornamental.

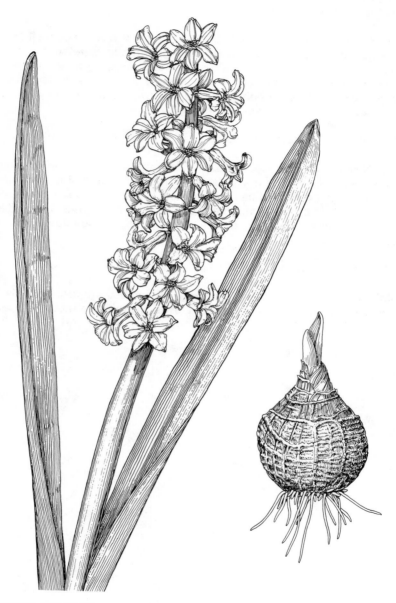

GARDEN HYACINTH   Note the large cluster of flowers on the seed stalk, the long, narrow, parallel-veined leaves, and the net-covered bulb of this attractive spring-flowering plant.

HYACINTHS

Garden Hyacinth
(Hyacinthus orientalis)

DESCRIPTION AND DISTRIBUTION: Hyacinths are bulbous perennial herbs in the lily family introduced from the Mediterranean region. Leaves are basal, long, and narrow. Flowers are white, yellow, pink, red, or blue in a cluster at the end of the seedstalk. Fruit is a 3-celled capsule filled with black seeds. Plants are grown in pots and gardens throughout the United States.

TOXIC PART: Bulbs.

POISONING: Garden hyacinth contains alkaloids that can be dangerous if eaten in quantity. The bulb is the most poisonous. It can also cause contact dermatitis in sensitive individuals.

SYMPTOMS: Intense stomach cramps, nausea, vomiting, and diarrhea.

COMMENT: The plants are cultivated as a source of perfume in France.

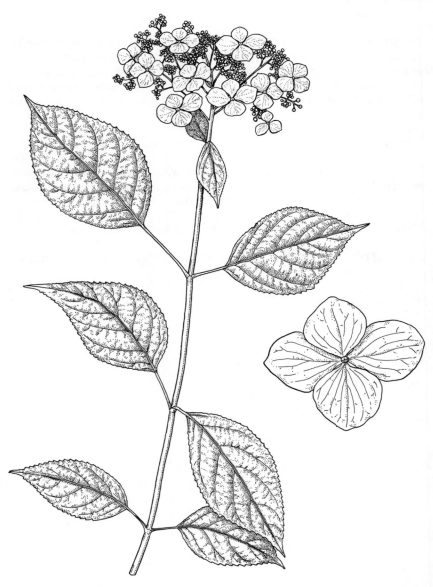

HYDRANGEA The clusters of colorful flowers and the oval toothed leaves are characteristic of this attractive ornamental shrub.

Hydrangeas
(Hydrangea sp.)

DESCRIPTION AND DISTRIBUTION: Hydrangeas are native and introduced deciduous and evergreen shrubs. Leaves are opposite and smooth-margined to toothed, rarely lobed. Flowers, which may be white, pink, lavender, or blue, are borne in clusters at the ends of branches or in leaf axils. Fruit is a capsule. Some species are native to the eastern United States, and various species are widely cultivated in the United States.

TOXIC PARTS: Entire plant.

POISONING: Under normal conditions these plants are nontoxic, but leaves and buds contain hydrangin, a cyanogenic glycoside, which under certain conditions can develop hydrocyanic acid and cause poisoning. However, symptoms are not typical of cyanide poisoning so other poisons may be involved. Poisoning may be expected from both wild and cultivated species.

SYMPTOMS: Nausea, vomiting, and diarrhea, which may be bloody.

COMMENTS: The roots have been used to produce a medicinal drug. A family in Florida was poisoned when children added hydrangea buds to a tossed salad.

IRIS   The complex colorful flower, the long, basal, parallel-veined leaves, the fleshy ringed rootstocks, the seedpods (lower right), and the seed (enlarged, lower left) are characteristic of this beautiful plant.

Irises

flags, fleur-de-lis *(Iris* sp.*)*

DESCRIPTION AND DISTRIBUTION: Irises are lily-like perennial herbs in the iris family, growing from thick creeping underground rootstocks. Leaves are long, narrow, and 2-ranked. Flowers are large and complex colorful structures in a wide range of colors — pink, blue, lilac, and purple to white, brown, yellow, orange, and almost black. Fruit is a 3-celled capsule containing numerous seeds. Native to the north temperate mountains and meadows, both wild and cultivated species are common in the United States.

TOXIC PARTS: Leaves and especially the rootstock.

POISONING: Wild and cultivated irises contain an irritating resinous substance irisin which acts on the intestinal tract, liver, and pancreas. Moderate amounts can cause severe digestive upset. Handling the rootstocks or leaves may also cause dermatitis.

SYMPTOMS: Burning, congestion, and severe pain in the intestinal tract; nausea and severe diarrhea.

COMMENTS: Cases of human poisoning are rare because of the bitter taste of the plant; however, children should be warned not to eat the fleshy parts of garden or wild irises. Most irises are grown as ornamentals, but several Old World species are used to produce orris, the dried powdered rootstock which has the odor of violets and is used in making perfume.

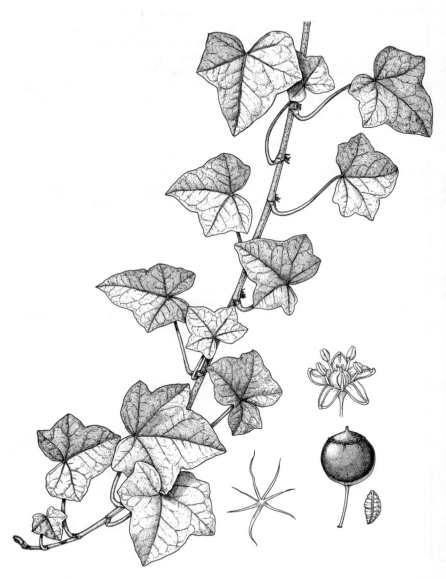

IVY Note the shiny 5-lobed leaves; the twining stems with root clusters for attachment; the flower, fruit, and seed (enlarged, lower right); and the star-shaped hairs (lower center) of this attractive plant.

IVIES

English Ivy
(Hedera helix) and other species

DESCRIPTION AND DISTRIBUTION: Ivies are evergreen and woody, climbing or creeping vines which are rarely shrublike. A member of the aralia family, they bear numerous short aerial roots. Leaves are leathery, alternate, usually palmately 5-lobed, bearing star-shaped hairs. Flowers are small and greenish and occur in many-flowered clusters. Fruits are 3- to 5-seeded black berries. A native of Europe, it is widely naturalized throughout the United States and planted indoors as an ornamental.

TOXIC PARTS: Berries and leaves.

POISONING: The toxin in this species is believed to be a saponic glycoside hederagenin. Children have been poisoned after ingestion of the berries, but the plant rarely produces berries.

SYMPTOMS: Excitement, difficulty in breathing, and coma. Other symptoms may include salivation, nausea, vomiting, abdominal pain, severe diarrhea, jaundice, headache, and fever.

COMMENT: Leaves of ivy cause dermatitis in some individuals, causing severe blisters and inflammation.

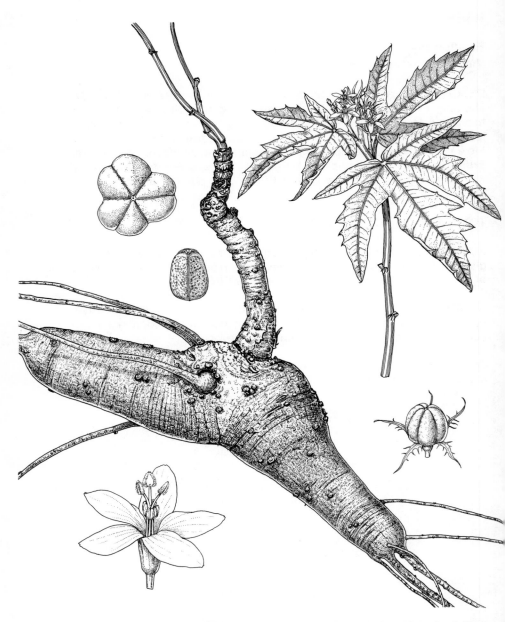

JATROPHA *(Jatropha macrorhiza)* **Note** the large thick root, the palmately divided leaves, the flower clusters, the flower (enlarged, lower left), the lobed seed pods (enlarged, upper left and lower right), and the seed (enlarged, left center) of this attractive desert plant.

Jatrophas
coral plants, physic nuts, barbados nuts *(Jatropha* sp.*)*

DESCRIPTION AND DISTRIBUTION: Jatrophas are tropical and sub-tropical herbs, shrubs, or trees in the spurge family, with milky or watery juice. Leaves are alternate and simple to divided. Flowers are yellow, purple, or scarlet with sexes in separate flowers. Fruit is a 3-lobed vari-ously colored capsule. Both native and introduced species are grown in the Southwest as ornamentals.

TOXIC PARTS: Entire plant, especially the seeds.

POISONING: The sap contains the toxalbumin curcin, a phytotoxin. Human poisoning is common, especially in children. Fruits are particu-larly attractive to children. Adults may be poisoned by overdoses of oil, which is used as a purgative, or from eating the thick roots or attractive seeds. As few as three seeds may cause severe symptoms. However, the seeds may be rendered non-toxic by roasting. Also, the plants are reported to cause insanity.

SYMPTOMS: Nausea, violent vomiting, abdominal pain, muscle cramps, bloody diarrhea, perspiration, dehydration, drowsiness, and coma. In severe cases, death may result. Non-lethal symptoms are rela-tively short-lived, clearing up within 24 hours.

COMMENTS: Jatrophas are one of the chief causes of poisoning in South Florida, and many cases of poisoning have been reported in the Southwest. Hairs on some species may cause dermatitis. On the other hand, jatrophas have many beneficial uses: the plants for medicinal pur-poses, the stems for production of rubber and for construction, the roots for the production of tannin and a red dye for tanning leather, and the seeds for production of oil. Also, it has been used as a fish poison and is reported to contain jatropham, a tumor-inhibiting agent.

95

JERUSALEM-CHERRY   Note the oblong, wavy-margined leaves, the white flowers (enlarged, lower left), and the attractive berries (enlarged, lower right) and seeds (enlarged, lower center) of this ornamental plant.

Jerusalem-Cherry
(Solanum pseudocapsicum)

DESCRIPTION AND DISTRIBUTION: Jerusalem-cherry is a smooth erect shrub belonging to the poisonous nightshade family. Leaves are oblong, pointed, glossy, and wavy. Flowers are white and usually borne singly or a few in the axils of the leaves. Fruits are round berries, either bright red or orange. Introduced from the Old World, plants are grown in pots throughout the United States at Christmas time for their showy berries. They are naturalized in the subtropical and tropical areas.

TOXIC PARTS: Entire plant, especially the leaves and unripened berries.

POISONING: The alkaloids solanine, solanidine, and solanocapsine have been isolated from the plants, so caution should be taken to prevent children from eating the berries or plants.

SYMPTOMS: Headache, stomach pain, subnormal temperature, vomiting, diarrhea, convulsions, respiratory and central nervous system depression, paralysis, dilated pupils, and loss of sensation. In severe cases, death may result.

COMMENTS: Solanine can be extremely toxic, and small amounts can be deadly. However, severe poisoning is rare because most cases result from eating the relatively non-toxic ripe berries.

CAROLINA JESSAMINE and STAR JASMINE   The leaves, flowers, and enlarged green and mature fruits and seed of Carolina jessamine are shown above; the leaves and flowers (single petal unrolled) of the star jasmine are below.

JESSAMINE, JASMINE

Carolina Jessamine
yellow jessamine, Carolina yellow jessamine, yellow jasmine
(Gelsemium sempervirens)

DESCRIPTION AND DISTRIBUTION: Carolina jessamine is a woody trailing or climbing evergreen vine in the logania family. Young stems are shiny red-brown, many-branched, and tangled. Leaves are opposite, simple, lance-shaped, and glossy with smooth margins. The fragrant yellow flowers are tubular with flared openings. Fruit is a flattened, 2-celled, beaked capsule. The plant is native to the southeastern United States and is commonly grown in the Southwest as an ornamental.

TOXIC PARTS: Entire plant.

POISONING: The alkaloids gelsemine and gelseminine are found throughout the plant with the greatest concentrations in the roots and nectar of the flowers. Children have been severely poisoned by chewing on the leaves and sucking the nectar from the flowers. Bees are poisoned by the nectar and persons may be poisoned by eating honey made from the flowers. Plants may also cause dermatitis.

SYMPTOMS: Profuse sweating, muscular weakness, convulsions, respiratory depression, and paralysis of the motor nerves. Death is possible through respiratory failure. Other symptoms may include nausea, vomiting, staggering, dilated pupils, pain above the eyes, and double vision.

COMMENTS: Medicinal drugs (sedatives) have been made from the rootstocks but overdoses are dangerous. Yellow jessamine is one of the most beautiful flowers of the Southeast and is the state flower of South Carolina. Unrelated genera called jessamine or jasmine that may also be poisonous are *Jasminum* (jasmine or jessamine), which belongs to the olive family, and *Trachelospermum* (star jasmine) and *Tabernaemontana* (crape jasmine), which belong to the dogbane family.

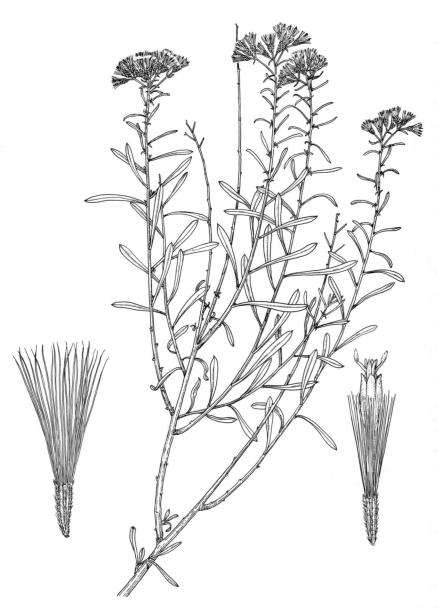

JIMMYWEED   The narrow pointed leaves, the clusters of yellow flower **heads** at the tips of the branches, and the flower (enlarged, lower right) and fruit (enlarged, lower left) with its crown of **bristles characterize** this plant.

Jimmyweed

rayless goldenrod *(Haplopappus heterophyllus)* and other species

DESCRIPTION AND DISTRIBUTION: Jimmyweed is a small bushy half-shrub in the sunflower family with narrow alternate and sticky leaves. It has clusters of small yellow flower-heads located at the tips of the stems. The plant is common on the desert plains and bottomlands of the Southwest.

TOXIC PARTS: Entire plant.

POISONING: The toxin in jimmyweed is the higher alcohol tremetol. It is transmitted to the milk of animals grazing on the plants and causes poisoning in humans known as "milk sickness." Poisoning is most common in late fall and winter but may occur at any time of the year.

SYMPTOMS: Nausea, severe vomiting, loss of appetite, constipation, weakness, tremors, jaundice due to liver damage, convulsions, and death. A decrease or absence of urination may accompany or follow kidney damage.

COMMENT: Jimmyweed is the species of this genus that is most frequently reported as poisonous to humans but burroweed *(Haplopappus tenuisectus)* and other species are also suspected.

MEXICAN JUMPING-BEAN   The leathery linear leaves, the long clusters of flowers with male flowers above and female flowers below, and the enlarged 2-valved fruit and oval seed (center) are characteristic of this unusual plant. The male flowers are shown, enlarged, lower left; the female flowers, enlarged, lower right.

JUMPING-BEANS

Mexican Jumping-Bean
Yerba-de-fleche *(Sapium biloculare)*

DESCRIPTION AND DISTRIBUTION: This Mexican jumping-bean is a deciduous milky-juiced shrub or small tree in the spurge family. Leaves are simple and alternate, leathery and linear. Flowers are fragrant, without petals, and borne in long clusters with male flowers above and female below. Fruit is a 2-valved rounded capsule. Plants are native to western Arizona, southeastern California, and northern Mexico.

TOXIC PART: Sap.

POISONING: The sap is reputedly very poisonous and plants cause sore eyes when burned for wood. Even sleeping under the trees of this plant is said to cause sore eyes. Also, Indians used the sap to poison arrows and stupefy fish.

SYMPTOMS: Undocumented except for sore eyes.

COMMENTS: The seeds are often infested with the larvae of a small moth which causes them to move around and even jump. The more common Mexican jumping-bean is *Sebastiana pavoniana,* another member of the spurge family that is more widespread but found only in Mexico. Other species of *Sapium* in South America are sources of rubber.

Junipers
(Juniperus sp.)

Junipers are native and introduced trees and shrubs widely grown as ornamentals and hedges. They contain volatile oils that are reported to cause stomach upset, diarrhea, convulsions, unconsciousness, dermatitis, edema, kidney damage, abortion, and even death when ingested or inhaled. However, the plants are extremely distasteful and are unlikely to be eaten in sufficient quantity to cause serious trouble.

LAMBSQUARTER Note the oval, wavy-margined, mealy-coated leaves, the small flowers clustered on the stem, and the seed (enlarged, upper left) of this weedy potherb.

Lambsquarter
goosefoot *(Chenopodium album)*

DESCRIPTION AND DISTRIBUTION: Lambsquarter is an annual weedy herb in the goosefoot family introduced from Europe. Leaves are oval to linear, simple, and mealy with entire to toothed margins. Flowers are small and green in clusters in the leaf axils or at the ends of branches. Plants are naturalized throughout most of North America.

TOXIC PARTS: Entire plant.

POISONING: Greens and seeds of lambsquarter have been used by Indians and pioneers as potherbs and for making mush and cakes even though it is a plant which frequently contains toxic quantities of nitrate and oxalic acid. Nitrate poisoning is almost exclusively a disease of livestock since man rarely eats enough of a given species to cause harm. If the diet is low in calcium, oxalic acid may produce a calcium deficiency with its complex effects.

SYMPTOMS: Symptoms of nitrate poisoning include headache, flushing of the skin, vomiting, dizziness, reduced blood pressure, bluish mucous membranes, collapse, coma, and respiratory paralysis, which can result in death. Symptoms of oxalic acid poisoning include excitement, convulsions, collapse, and kidney failure.

COMMENTS: A related species *(Chenopodium ambrosioides)* is cultivated for its oil of chenopodium which is used to kill or eject intestinal worms. Its medicinal use can cause poisoning resulting in nausea, vomiting, headache, acute depression, kidney damage, and convulsions.

LANTANA   The oval, toothed, and veiny leaves; the square prickly stems; the terminal flower clusters; and the black berries are characteristic of this attractive ornamental shrub.

Lantanas

(Lantana sp.)

DESCRIPTION AND DISTRIBUTION: Lantanas are mostly shrubs of the vervain family introduced from tropical and subtropical America. They have square twigs with a few scattered spines. Leaves are simple, opposite or whorled, and oval-shaped with toothed margins. Flowers are white, yellow, orange, red, or blue; small and tubular, they occur in flat-topped clusters. Fruit is berrylike with a hard seed, turning blue-black at maturity. The plant is cultivated as an ornamental shrub in the warmer parts of the United States and as a potted plant in the North. They have escaped along stream bottoms in some parts of the Southwest.

TOXIC PARTS: All parts, especially the green berries.

POISONING: The fruits contain an alkaloid lantanin or lantadene A. The green unripened fruit is the most dangerous, especially to children. However, birds eat the berries, seemingly without harm.

SYMPTOMS: Stomach and intestinal irritation, bloody diarrhea, vomiting, muscular weakness, jaundice, and circulatory collapse. Death is possible but not common.

COMMENTS: The plants are native to Florida and are considered a major cause of human poisoning in that state. Also, the plant foliage can cause photosensitization in livestock and pets, and dermatitis in humans.

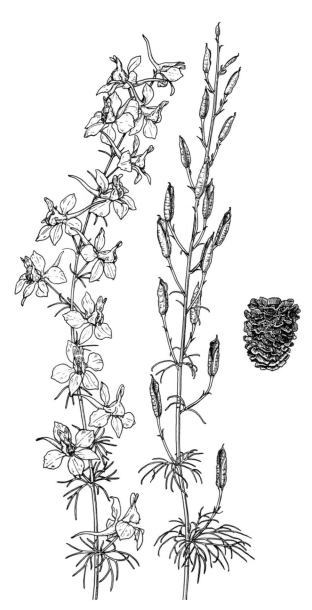

CULTIVATED LARKSPUR These plants have finely divided leaves, blue to white or pink spurred flowers, a dry splitting seed pod, and a rough seed (enlarged, right center).

Larkspurs

delphiniums *(Delphinium* sp.*)*

DESCRIPTION AND DISTRIBUTION: Larkspurs are tall or short, annual or perennial herbs of the crowfoot family that grow in the North Temperate Zone. Leaves are palmately divided into numerous lobes. The showy flowers are usually blue with one of the sepals forming a distinctive spur that projects backward. The flowers are borne in elongated clusters at the ends of tall flower stalks. Some cultivated flowers are double and more than one color. Seeds are enclosed in a 3-celled capsule. Cultivated varieties are widely grown in flower gardens; native plants are most abundant in the forests and meadows of the West.

TOXIC PARTS: Entire plant.

POISONING: Larkspurs contain the alkaloids delphinine, delphinoidine, ajacine, and others, mostly in the seeds and young plants. Danger decreases as plants mature but alkaloids remain concentrated in the seeds. Powdered larkspur seed is used in some commercial lice remedies and may present a danger to pets and humans.

SYMPTOMS: Burning sensation of the mouth and skin, nervousness, headache, weakness, prickling of the skin, low blood pressure, nausea, vomiting, depression, weak pulse, and convulsions. If eaten in large quantities, death may occur within less than 6 hours.

COMMENTS: Since the plants are not normally eaten by humans, the principal danger to man results from experimentation by adults or accidental consumption by children. Larkspur is also suspected of causing dermatitis in susceptible persons.

LICHENS

Lichens

ground lichens *(Parmelia molliuscula)* and other species

Lichens are toxic to man and animal, producing difficulty in walking, paralysis, and even death when eaten in large quantities. Under natural conditions, poisoning of animals is mild. If used by man for emergency food, the lichens should be cooked in water to remove the mild toxins.

GLORIOSA LILY Lance-shaped leaves elongated into tendrils, colorful upside-down flowers, and thick tubers (lower right) characterize this attractive plant.

LILIES

Gloriosa Lilies
climbing lilies, glory lilies *(Gloriosa* sp.*)*

DESCRIPTION AND DISTRIBUTION: Gloriosa lilies are slender herbs or vines in the lily family that grow from a thick tuber. The lance-shaped leaves are elongated into tendrils. The red and yellow lilylike flowers are borne singly and upside down in the leaf axils, with the colorful segments reflexed or spreading. The fruit is an oblong capsule. Introduced from Africa and Asia, they are frequently planted outside in Florida and Hawaii and as potted houseplants elsewhere in the United States.

TOXIC PARTS: Entire plants, particularly the tubers.

POISONING: The stems, leaves, seeds, and tubers contain colchicine and other alkaloids which are extremely poisonous and can cause death in human beings.

SYMPTOMS: Numbness of lips, tongue, and throat; burning in the mouth and stomach; vomiting; diarrhea; difficulty in breathing; shock; convulsions; and death due to respiratory failure.

COMMENTS: Death has occurred within 4 hours after ingestion of tubers. The tuber and its extracted latex have been used in folk medicine in Asia and Africa with overdoses resulting in death.

LILY-OF-THE-VALLEY The delicate white fragrant flowers (enlarged, right), the long lance-shaped leaves, and the horizontal rootstocks are characteristic of this hardy ornamental.

Lily-of-the-Valley
(Convallaria majalis)

DESCRIPTION AND DISTRIBUTION: Lily-of-the-valley is a low-grow-ing herbaceous perennial of the lily family which grows from a running rootstock forming beds of flowers. The leaves are basal, broad, and parallel-veined. The white, fragrant, and attractive bell-shaped flowers grow in nodding one-sided clusters above the leaves. Fruit is a red berry which seldom forms. An introduction from Eurasia, it is natural-ized in eastern North America and is grown in pots and flower gardens elsewhere.

TOXIC PARTS: Entire plant.

POISONING: The leaves, roots, flowers, and fruits contain the cardiac glycoside convallatoxin and other glycosides that act as strong heart stimulents, much like digitalis. Lily-of-the-valley is less poisonous than other cardiac glycoside plants due to the fact that it is less potent or is more distasteful.

SYMPTOMS: Loss of appetite, irregular heartbeat, nausea, vomiting, diarrhea, headache, dizziness, hallucinations, depression, and heart failure. Adults receiving overdoses of digitalis medication, or children accidentally taking the sweet-tasting preparations suffer similar effects.

COMMENTS: The dried rhizomes have medicinal properties and the aromatic flowers are used in making perfume. A related species or variety *(Convallaria montana)* is native or naturalized in the high moun-tains of the eastern United States.

CARDINAL FLOWER Distinctive red 2-lipped tubular flowers and lance-shaped leaves are characteristic of this tall colorful herb. At right center the enlarged seed capsule and pitted seed are shown.

LOBELIAS
cardinal flowers, Indian-tobaccos

Cardinal Flower
(Lobelia cardinalis) and other species

DESCRIPTION AND DISTRIBUTION: Lobelias are erect, mostly unbranched annual or perennial herbs (or sometimes woody plants) of the lobelia family, native to the tropical and warm temperate regions. Leaves are lance-shaped, simple, and alternate. Several species have beautiful red, blue, or white, tubular 2-lipped flowers which are solitary or borne in terminal clusters. Fruit is a 2-valved capsule. Native species are found throughout the United States. Southwestern species, including cardinal flower, are found in moist forests, meadows, and along streams, and are frequently grown as ornamentals in flower gardens.

TOXIC PARTS: Entire plant.

POISONING: All parts of the plant contain lobeline, lobelamine, and numerous other alkaloids. Most cases of poisoning in earlier times were the result of overdoses of homemade medicines used in the treatment of laryngitis and spasmodic asthma.

SYMPTOMS: Nausea, vomiting, dizziness, headache, sweating, exhaustion, weakness, lowered temperature, prostration, feeble pulse, dilated pupils, abdominal pain, stupor, tremors, convulsions, respiratory failure, coma, and sometimes death.

COMMENTS: Lobeline has been used as an emetic, respiratory stimulant, and expectorant in the past, but now it is administered as a deterrent to tobacco smoking. Indian tobacco *(Lobelia inflata),* an eastern North American species, is the species most used as a commercial source of drugs. An interesting contradiction is that Indians used to smoke the dried leaves like tobacco. The plants are also suspected of causing dermatitis in some persons.

BLUE LOCO *(Astragalus lentiginosus* var. *diphysus)*　The long pinnately divided leaves; the clusters of pea-shaped blue flowers (enlarged, right); the inflated, often speckled pods (lower right); and seed (enlarged, right center) are characteristic of this dangerous plant.

LOCOWEEDS, CRAZYWEEDS
rattleweeds, locos, poison-vetches

Locoweeds
(Astragalus sp.)

Crazyweeds
(Oxytropis sp.)

DESCRIPTION AND DISTRIBUTION: The locoweeds and closely related crazyweeds are native herbaceous perennials in the legume family that vary from erect to prostrate in growth form. Leaves are usually hairy and pinnately divided. The pea-shaped flowers are borne in clusters in the axils of the leaves or at the top of flower stalks. Seeds are borne in small to large inflated pods. Species of these genera are common throughout the Southwest numbering over 100 species.

TOXIC PART: Leaves.

POISONING: Locoweeds and crazyweeds contain alkaloidlike substances that cause serious loss of livestock while most human poisonings are attributed to accumulations of selenium that occur in plants growing on soils naturally high in selenium. The alkaloids can also cause serious poisoning of humans.

SYMPTOMS: Typical symptoms of chronic selenium poisoning include pallor, garlicky odor to the breath, metallic taste, stomach and intestinal disturbances, irritation of the nose and throat, inflammation of the eyes, dermatitis, drowsiness, constriction of the chest, and anemia. Also, brain damage may result from smoking the plants.

COMMENTS: Since locoweeds are seldom eaten by humans, they don't present a serious threat to man. However, other crops, such as the cereals, when growing on seleniferous soils do accumulate selenium and present a serious hazard.

BLACK LOCUST Note the pendulous flower clusters and flower (enlarged, upper left), the pinnately divided leaves, and the flattened pod and enlarged seed (lower right) of this popular ornamental tree.

LOCUSTS

Black Locust

(Robinia pseudoacacia) and other species

DESCRIPTION AND DISTRIBUTION: Black locust is a small tree in the legume family with pinnately divided deciduous leaves, spiny twigs, and black bark. The showy pea-shaped white flowers hang in pendulous clusters; the seeds are borne in flat reddish legume pods. It is a native of the eastern United States and Canada but is widely planted as an ornamental in the West.

TOXIC PARTS: Bark, foliage, and seeds.

POISONING: The inner bark, young leaves, and seeds contain the phytotoxin robin and the toxic glycoside robitin. Children may be poisoned by sucking the fresh twigs, eating the inner bark, or eating the seeds.

SYMPTOMS: Nausea, vomiting, diarrhea, weak pulse, weakness, depression, and coldness of arms and legs. Death in humans from eating black locust is unlikely.

COMMENT: New Mexico locust *(Robinia neomexicana)*, a native western shrub with spiny twigs, pinnate leaves, and rose-colored flowers, is also suspected of being poisonous to man.

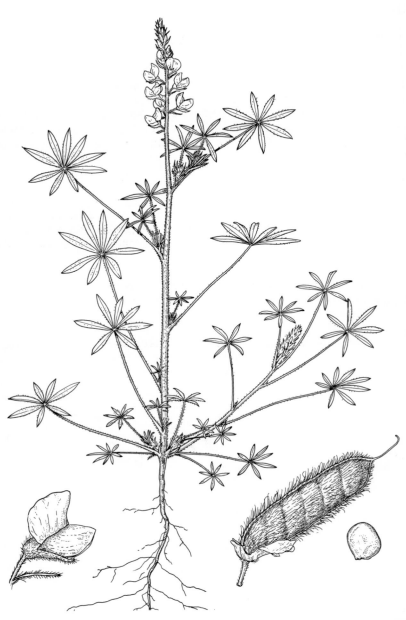

FEW-FLOWERED LUPINE *(Lupinus sparsiflorus)* Note the digitately divided leaves, the hairy foliage, the pea-shaped flower (lower left), and the flattened hairy seed pod and seed (enlarged, lower right) of this unusual plant.

Lupines

lupins, bluebonnets *(Lupinus* sp.)

DESCRIPTION AND DISTRIBUTION: Lupines are annual or perennial herbs in the pea family with wide distribution, being most numerous in western North America. Leaves are alternate and digitately divided. The blue, white, red, or yellow flowers are showy and pea-shaped, borne in clusters at the ends of stems. The seeds are borne in flattened pods; the pods are often constricted between the seeds. At maturity the pods divide and form two spirally coiled segments. Lupines are found throughout the Southwest but are most important on foothill and mountain ranges. Many are cultivated as ornamentals.

TOXIC PARTS: Entire plant, especially the seeds.

POISONING: Lupines contain lupinine and related toxic alkaloids. The seeds and pods are most dangerous, and both young and dried plants may be poisonous. Cultivated varieties have poisoned children, but cases are apparently rare.

SYMPTOMS: Weak pulse, respiratory depression, convulsions, and paralysis.

COMMENTS: Not all species are poisonous. Lupines may contaminate grain and flour made from improperly cleaned grain. Consumption of lupine by cows has caused birth deformities in calves and might have similar effects in humans.

MANIHOT *(Manihot angustiloba)*   Note the deeply lobed, palmately divided leaves, the male flowers (above) and the fruits (below) on the seed stalk (lower right), and the seed and fruit (enlarged, far right) of this southwestern species. The large, deeply buried, tuberous root is not shown.

Manihots

cassavas, tapiocas, maniocs *(Manihot* sp.*)*

DESCRIPTION AND DISTRIBUTION: Manihots are native to tropical North and South America, including the southwestern United States. Plants are herbs, shrubs, or trees in the spurge family with milky juice and tuberous roots. Leaves are alternate and usually palmately divided. Flowers are without petals, with sexes in separate flowers. The fruits are 3-lobed capsules.

TOXIC PART: Roots.

POISONING: The large tuberous roots of manihot *(Manihot esculenta)* when cooked are used extensively for making cassava, tapioca, starch, and other food products. However, the raw roots of some species of manihot contain amygdalin, a soluble cyanogenetic glycoside that breaks down into hydrocyanic acid, which can cause cyanide poisoning to those unfamiliar with proper preparation of the roots. The oil of the seeds is both an emetic and cathartic similar to castor oil.

SYMPTOMS: Symptoms of mild doses are weakness, giddiness, head-ache, nausea, vomiting, and rapid pulse. Lethal doses cause muscular incoordination, convulsions, and coma. Death can occur within minutes. A diagnostic symptom is the odor of almond on the breath.

COMMENTS: With the present well-established practices of peeling and heating the roots to drive off the cyanide, there is little danger of poisoning. *Manihot glaziovii* is the tree that produces the ceara rubber of commerce.

MARIHUANA Note the palmately divided toothed leaves, the male flower (**upper left**), the female flower (upper right), the female flower with bracts removed (right center), and seed (enlarged, lower right) of this controversial drug plant.

Marihuana

marijuana, hemp, hashish, Mary Jane, pot, grass *(Cannabis sativa)*

DESCRIPTION AND DISTRIBUTION: Marihuana is a tall coarse annual herb in the hemp family, introduced from temperate Asia. The leaves are long-stalked and palmately divided into 3 to 7 narrow and pointed, toothed leaflets. Flowers are small, green, and clustered in the leaf axils. Male and female flowers are on separate plants. Flowers, leaves, and stems are covered with hairs which exude a sticky resin from which marihuana is obtained. It is a widely naturalized weed in temperate North America and is cultivated in warmer regions.

TOXIC PARTS: Entire plant, especially the leaves, flowering parts, sap, and resinous secretions.

POISONING: The toxins are various narcotic resins, mainly THC (tetrahydrocannabinol) and related compounds which produce hallucinogenic effects. The amount of resinoid in the various plant parts varies with plant variety, sex of plant, geographic location, and growing season. Toxic substances are highest in plants grown in warm climates or seasons and in female plants. Poisoning may result from drinking the extract, chewing the plant parts, or smoking "reefers." Effects of these plants have been known for more than 2,000 years.

SYMPTOMS: Exhilaration, hallucinations, delusions, mental confusion, dilated pupils, blurred vision, poor coordination, weakness, stupor, and coma (if large doses have been consumed). Death may result from its depressing effect on the heartbeat. Other symptoms include craving for sweets, increased appetite, dryness of mouth, inflamed eyes, anxiety, aggressiveness, sleep disturbance, tremors, decreased sexual potency, feeling of contentment, increased but faulty perception and imagination, loss of initiative, reduction of will power and concentration, and impairment of lung function.

COMMENTS: The inner bark contains the tough hemp fibers used in making rope, the fruits are used as bird seed and to produce a useful drying oil, and the dried flowering and fruiting tops produce drugs such as marihuana. Federal and state laws prohibit the possession of living or dried parts of marihuana both in the United States and Canada.

MESCAL BEAN Pinnately divided leaves, clusters of purplish pea-like flowers (enlarged, left center), constricted pods (lower center), and bright red seeds (enlarged, lower left) characterize this attractive but dangerous plant.

MESCAL BEANS

Mescal Bean
frijolito *(Sophora secundiflora)* and other species

DESCRIPTION AND DISTRIBUTION: Mescal bean is an evergreen shrub or small tree in the pea family. Leaves are pinnately divided into 5 to 13 oblong leaflets. Leaflets have silky hairs on the underside and a shiny yellow-green surface above. Pea-like flowers are violet-blue and fragrant, growing in dense one-sided terminal clusters. Seeds are bright red in a woody pod. Plants are native to southwestern Texas, southern New Mexico, and northern Mexico, and cultivated as ornamentals elsewhere in the Southwest. Plants grow best on limestone soils.

TOXIC PARTS: Entire plant, especially the seed.

POISONING: The entire plant contains cytisine and other poisonous alkaloids. One seed thoroughly chewed is sufficient to cause the death of a child, but the hard unbroken whole seeds pass through the digestive tract without harm. Mature foliage is toxic to livestock and may be harmful to humans if eaten or used to make tea. Several other southwestern species of *Sophora* also contain toxic alkaloids but are apparently less toxic than mescal bean.

SYMPTOMS: Nausea, vomiting, diarrhea, excitement, delirium, hallucinations, coma, and death. Non-lethal doses may cause a deep sleep that lasts for 2 to 3 days.

COMMENTS: The seeds have long been used in medicine as a narcotic and hallucinatory drug by the Indians in Mexico and the Southwest, and have been used extensively to make necklaces. Chewing the necklace beans can cause poisoning.

OAK MISTLETOE *(Phorodendron coryae)* The paired oval leaves, the flowers embedded in the flower stalk (upper right), and the white sticky berries and grooved seeds
(enlarged, lower center) are characteristic of this parasitic plant.

Mistletoes
(Phoradendron sp.*)*

DESCRIPTION AND DISTRIBUTION: Mistletoes are parasitic plants in the mistletoe family that grow on trees and shrubs. Plants may or may not contain chlorophyll. Leaves are opposite and vary from scales to well-developed, simple, oblong, and leathery leaves. Flowers are small and usually embedded in the flower stalk. Fruits are small white berries with sticky pulp. Various species of American mistletoes are found throughout the United States, Mexico, and Canada.

TOXIC PARTS: All parts, especially the berries.

POISONING: Berries contain the toxic amines beta-phenylethylamine and tyramine. Persons have been poisoned by eating or making tea from the berries.

SYMPTOMS: Stomach and intestinal pains, diarrhea, slow pulse, and collapse. Death may occur within a few hours. Other symptoms include nausea, vomiting, nervousness, difficult breathing, delirium, hallucinations, dilation of pupils, abortion, convulsions, and heart failure.

COMMENTS: Since mistletoe is a favorite Christmas decoration, care should be taken to keep the berries out of reach of children. The common American mistletoe is *Phoradendron serotinum,* formerly *Phoradendron flavescens;* the European species is *Viscum album.* An extract of the leaves of mistletoe is toxic to mosquitoes. Indians chewed the leaves for toothache, and the plant has been used as a stimulant in cardiac treatment.

MOLDS

Molds, produced by numerous fungi in grains, forage, legumes, and cottonseed meal, have resulted in extensive poisonings of livestock and pets in the United States but apparently not in man. However, human poisonings have been reported in Russia and Japan. A mold, *Aspergillus flavus,* produces aflatoxin which causes liver cancer and chromosome changes in animals. Although not conclusively demonstrated, animal studies indicate that aflatoxin can produce similar effects in man. Therefore, ingestion of moldy foods such as bread, grains, peanuts, sweet potatoes, and milk should be avoided.

WESTERN MONKSHOOD   The hooded, dark blue flowers, the palmately lobed leaves, the beaked capsule, and rough seed (enlarged, lower right) are characteristic of this dangerous plant.

MONKSHOODS

Western Monkshood
aconite, wolfsbane *(Aconitum columbianum)* and other species

DESCRIPTION AND DISTRIBUTION: Western monkshood is a perennial herb in the buttercup or crowfoot family growing up to 2 m tall. It resembles larkspur except flowers are without spurs. Leaves are alternate, petioled, and palmately divided into segments with pointed tips. Both petals and sepals of flowers are generally dark blue and irregular, the upper sepal forming a prominent hood. The seeds are enclosed in a short beaked capsule. Plants grow in rich moist soil in meadows and along streams in the western mountains from Arizona northward into Canada.

TOXIC PARTS: All parts, especially roots and seeds.

POISONING: Monkshood contains several monobasic alkaloids, including aconine and aconitine. Death in humans has occurred from eating the plant or ingesting extracts made from it. Small amounts can be lethal. Toxicity varies with the climatic conditions under which plants are grown. Plants are most toxic in the preflowering stage.

SYMPTOMS: Aconite poisoning in humans is intense. Symptoms are burning sensation of the mouth and skin, nausea, intense vomiting and diarrhea, muscular weakness and spasms, weak and irregular pulse, prickling of the skin, paralysis of the respiratory system, dimness of vision, low blood pressure, convulsions, and death within a few hours.

COMMENTS: European monkshood is the source of the powerful heart stimulant aconite. The roots of monkshood have been mistaken for horseradish and have caused poisoning. However, it will not normally be eaten except by experimenting adults or small children.

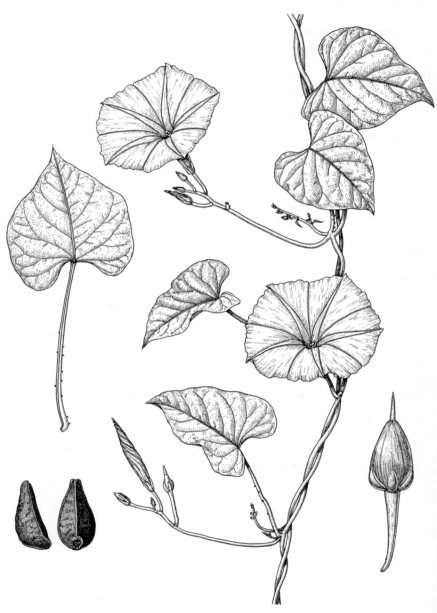

MORNING-GLORY Colorful trumpet-shaped flowers, heart-shaped leaves, and the seed capsule (enlarged, lower right) and seeds (enlarged, lower left) characterize this colorful vine.

Morning-Glory

heavenly blue, pearly gates, flying saucers, wedding bells, summer skies, blue star *(Ipomoea tricolor,* formerly *Ipomoea violacea)*

DESCRIPTION AND DISTRIBUTION: This member of the morning-glory family is a stout, twining, and glabrous perennial herb introduced from tropical America. Leaves are large, heart-shaped, and thickish. Flowers are tubular with flared openings and are varicolored from dark blue to white and sometimes rose-lavender. They are borne singly or in clusters in the axils of the leaves. Seeds are borne in a 4- to 6-valved capsule. These colorful flowers are widely grown as ornamentals, indoors in pots and outside on trellises. Propagation in Arizona is restricted because it becomes a weed in irrigated croplands.

TOXIC PART: Seeds.

POISONING: Seeds contain amides of lysergic acid which are related to LSD (lysergic acid diethylamide) and produce hallucinogenic reactions when eaten in quantity (50 to 500 seeds eaten whole or powdered and soaked in cold water, strained, and drunk).

SYMPTOMS: Hallucinations, panic, detachment, incoherent speech, cold hands and feet, nausea, vomiting, laughing and crying jags, strong body odor, mental disorder, and suicidal attempts.

COMMENTS: The above species was used by the Aztecs as a hallucinogen in religious ceremonies and in medicine. Other common ornamental species of *Ipomoea* grown in the United States have no hallucinogenic properties.

Although not illegal, hallucinogenic morning-glory seeds are not as popular as LSD or marijuana because they are only about 1/10 as potent as LSD and are generally hard to find in large quantities. Another hallucinogenic plant, *Rivea corymbosa,* known as ololiuqui in Mexico, is not cultivated north of Mexico.

Recent studies indicate that morning-glory may be a source of non-cancerous dyes for use in coloring foods.

MULBERRIES   Note the simple, toothed to lobed leaves, the male flower clusters and enlarged flower (upper right), the female flower cluster and female flower (enlarged, lower right), and the berry and seed (enlarged, lower left) of these plants. The major difference between the red and white mulberry is the color of the fruit, as the names indicate.

MULBERRIES

Red Mulberry
(Morus rubra)

White Mulberry
(Morus alba)

DESCRIPTION AND DISTRIBUTION: Mulberries are trees in the mulberry family growing up to 25 m in height. Leaves are alternate, ovate, sharply-toothed, and sometimes lobed. Male and female flowers are borne on separate plants in dense clusters in the axils of the leaves. Fruit of red mulberry is a red to purple, nearly round, compound berry; white mulberry is white, pinkish, or blackish-purple. Red mulberry is native to the rich bottomlands of central and eastern United States and is grown as an ornamental elsewhere. White mulberry is a native of China cultivated and escaped throughout the United States.

TOXIC PARTS: Green berries and sap from leaves and stems.

POISONING: The unripe fruits and milky sap from the leaves and stems of red mulberry are reported to contain unknown toxic substances that can cause dermatitis, hallucinations, and disturbance of the central nervous system. The toxic nature of white mulberry is unreported.

SYMPTOMS: Hallucinations, contact dermatitis, stimulation of the central nervous system, and upset stomach.

COMMENTS: The ripe fruits are eaten widely by humans and wildlife, especially birds. The fibrous bark was used by early Indians to make cloth. The white mulberry was imported by the pioneers to provide food for silkworms used for the production of silk.

FLY AMANITA Wide red to yellow cap, white gills, and whitish stalk with wavy "skirt" and bulbous base are characteristic of this mushroom.

MUSHROOMS

Fly Amanita
fly agaric, fly mushroom *(Amanita muscaria)*

DESCRIPTION AND DISTRIBUTION: Fly amanita is a mushroom with a 5 to 25 cm wide red to yellow cap, with white scales and whitish stalk 10 to 20 cm high. Both the gills and spores are white. In the Southwest it is found growing in circular groups (fairy rings) in the woods and meadows of pine, aspen, and spruce-fir forests. It lives in the soil humus and is attached to the roots of trees by a mass of filaments (mycorrhizae).

TOXIC PARTS: Entire plant.

POISONING: Fly amanita contains the poisons ibotenic acid, muscimol and other related compounds. These are hallucinogenic compounds that act on the nervous system. Symptoms usually occur within a few minutes to 2 hours. All but a very few persons recover rather quickly. Recent studies show that this mushroom contains only minute amounts of the toxin muscarine which was first discovered in and named after this species.

SYMPTOMS: Deathlike sleep, incoordination, derangement of senses, manic behavior, delirium, hearing of voices, seeing of colored visions, feeling of elation, and exaggerated physical activity. Also, explosive diarrhea, profuse sweating, and dizziness may occur. Effects are severe but rarely fatal.

COMMENTS: This plant is called fly amanita because mushrooms left in water or an open dish attract flies which are stunned or killed. A derivative of muscimol is being used as a pesticide in Japan and an extract of ibotenic acid is a flavor enhancer for food.

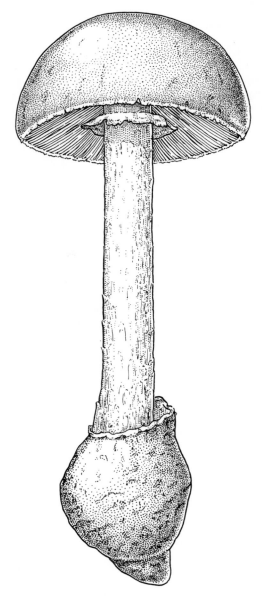

DESTROYING-ANGEL The long white stalk with bulbous base, the "skirt" on the upper part of the stalk, and the white oval cap are characteristic of this mushroom.

MUSHROOMS

Destroying-Angel

death cup, deadly amanita, white amanita *(Amanita verna)*

DESCRIPTION AND DISTRIBUTION: This species of the group of destroying angel mushrooms is chalky white and has a bulbous base. It occurs in open woods throughout the United States and Canada, with the exception of the Pacific coast. They are rarely found in lawns or meadows.

TOXIC PARTS: Entire plant.

POISONING: The poisons in destroying angel mushrooms are the complex polypeptides (or cyclopeptides) amanitin and possibly phalloidin. They cause the more deadly type of mushroom poisoning.

SYMPTOMS: Symptoms do not usually appear until 6 to 24 hours after ingestion. They include sudden and severe abdominal pain, profuse vomiting, diarrhea, distorted vision, excessive thirst, circulatory failure, prostration, coma, and death. Death may occur within 48 hours or the effects may last 6 to 8 days. Attacks may be interrupted by periods of remission. Recovery, if it occurs, may require up to a month. Permanent liver, kidney, and heart damage may result from non-lethal cases.

COMMENTS: Only experts can identify non-poisonous mushrooms, so don't gamble with your life by eating wild ones. The mortality rate is high; one or two mushrooms, raw or cooked, may prove fatal.

GREENGILL LEPIOTA The large, thick, umbrella-like scaly cap, and the white stalk (sometimes tinged with brown) are characteristic of this mushroom.

MUSHROOMS

Greengill Lepiota
Morgan lepiota, greenspored mushroom *(Chlorophyllum molybdites,* formerly *Lepiota morgani)*

DESCRIPTION AND DISTRIBUTION: Greengill lepiota is a large mushroom with a thick white scaly cap 10 to 30 cm wide and a white stalk (sometimes tinged with brown) up to 20 cm long. Gills and spores are greenish when mature, later turning dark brown. It has a small ring around the upper part of the stalk and is without a bulbous base. It is common in the western and southern states. In the Southwest it grows from August through October in lawns, fields, and pastures on organic soils in circular groups (fairy rings) up to 13 m across.

TOXIC PARTS: Entire plant.

POISONING: Lepiota contains gastrointestinal irritants and other toxins which cause gastrointestinal distress if eaten raw or improperly prepared or in large quantities. The toxin is a protein, and heating in water for 30 minutes at 70°C inactivates it. In severe cases, victims require hospitalization.

SYMPTOMS: These are strong purgatives and can cause nausea, weakness, faintness, chills, vomiting, cramps, and diarrhea (sometimes bloody) which may persist for two days or longer. Symptoms normally subside in 3 to 4 hours, and recovery is complete in a day or two. There is no involvement of the liver, kidneys or nervous system.

COMMENTS: This species causes many illnesses each year but few deaths are recorded. There are some edible species of *Lepiota,* but there is too much risk in trying to identify the edible forms.

BLACK MUSTARD   Note the dissected and toothed leaves, the terminal flower clusters, the slender constricted seed pod, and the seed (enlarged, lower right) of this mustard-producing plant.

MUSTARDS

Black Mustard
(Brassica nigra) and other species

DESCRIPTION AND DISTRIBUTION: Mustards of the genus *Brassica* are wild or cultivated, native or introduced. Mustards are annual, biennial, or perennial broad-leaved herbs or small shrubs. Leaves are variously toothed to pinnately divided. Flowers are yellow in long terminal clusters; seeds are usually in long slender constricted pods. Mainly of Old World origin, various species are found throughout the United States.

TOXIC PARTS: The roots and seeds are the most dangerous.

POISONING: The most important poisonous principle is mustard oil containing isothiocyanate and beta phenyl isothiocyanate. In pure form a single drop of oil of mustard in the eye can cause blindness. Various members of the mustard family, if eaten raw and in quantity, can cause severe irritation of the mucous membranes in the intestinal tract. In addition, mustards may accumulate dangerous levels of nitrate and produce goiter and anemia in experimental animals.

SYMPTOMS: Vomiting (sometimes bloody) and diarrhea.

COMMENTS: Various mustards are widely used for food and seasoning. They include black mustard, broccoli, cauliflower, cabbage, turnip, rutabaga, Brussels sprouts, radish, horseradish, rape, kale, and cress. Black mustard seed is a major source of table mustard.

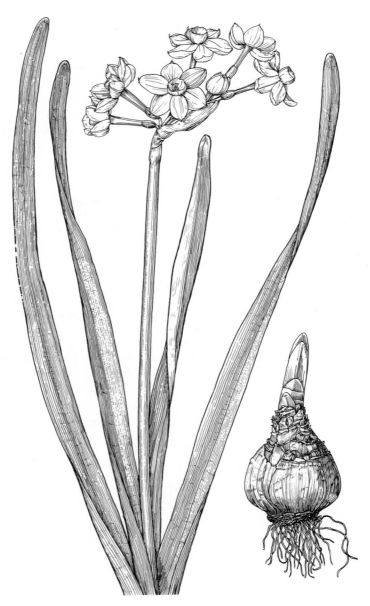

NARCISSUS The many white and/or yellow flowers at the end of the flower stalk, the long narrow leaves, and the scaly bulb (lower right) characterize this popular spring-flowering herb.

Narcissus

polyanthus narcissus, jonquil *(Narcissus tazetta),* and other species

DESCRIPTION AND DISTRIBUTION: Narcissus is a spring-flowering bulbous herb of the amaryllis family, introduced from the Mediterranean area. Leaves are basal, long, narrow, and parallel-veined. Flowers are 4 to 8 on a stalk, yellow or white, with the fused petals forming a ring at the end of a short tube. Fruit is a lobed capsule. They may be grown outdoors or as house plants.

TOXIC PART: Bulbs.

POISONING: The poisonous principle is unknown, but is possibly an alkaloid. Even small amounts of the bulbs may cause poisoning if eaten. The plants may also cause contact dermatitis in sensitive individuals.

SYMPTOMS: Severe digestive upset including nausea, vomiting, and diarrhea; nervous symptoms (such as trembling or convulsions), and in some cases death.

COMMENT: The bulbs of these plants should always be regarded as dangerous, especially to children.

BLACK NIGHTSHADE Note the entire to lobed leaves, the axillary flower clusters, the flower (enlarged, right), the clusters of berries, the berry (enlarged, left), and the seed (enlarged, lower center) of this dangerous herb.

NIGHTSHADES

Black Nightshade
common nightshade, poisonberry *(Solanum nigrum)*

DESCRIPTION AND DISTRIBUTION: Black nightshade is a prostrate or erect annual in the nightshade family. Leaves are simple, ovate, alternate, and entire or lobed. Flowers are small, white, and star-shaped in axillary drooping clusters. Fruits are round, with purple or black berries with many seeds. Plants are weeds introduced throughout the United States and southern Canada.

TOXIC PARTS: Leaves and unripe berries.

POISONING: The plants contain the glyco-alkaloid solanine. The alkaloid is most highly concentrated in the unripe berries which are very attractive to children. Solanine is extremely toxic; even small amounts can be deadly. All species of nightshade should be considered poisonous. The plants are also reported to contain saponin and atropine and to accumulate high levels of nitrate.

SYMPTOMS: Headache, stomach pain, vomiting, diarrhea, dilated pupils, subnormal temperature, shock, abdominal pain, circulatory and respiratory depression, loss of sensation, and paralysis. Death may occur in severe cases due to respiratory paralysis.

COMMENTS: The completely ripe fruits of nightshade contain the least solanine of any part of the plant, and can be used to make pies and jellies; berries of the cultivated crosses such as sunberry or wonderberry *(Solanum burbankii)* are often used. Boiling apparently destroys the toxic principles: young shoots and leaves have been cooked and eaten like spinach, after draining the cooking water.

SILVERLEAF NIGHTSHADE   Note the spiny leaves and stems, the wheel-shaped flowers, and the varicolored fruit and seed (enlarged, upper right) of this common weed.

NIGHTSHADES

Silverleaf Nightshade
white horsenettle, trompillo *(Solanum elaeagnifolium)*

DESCRIPTION AND DISTRIBUTION: Silverleaf nightshade is an upright, spiny perennial herb of the nightshade family with creeping rootstocks. Leaves are simple, oblong, silvery, thick, and spiny with wavy margins. The deep violet or blue flowers are 5-lobed, wheel-shaped, and showy. The fruit is a mottled or striped berry which becomes yellow or orange-yellow at maturity. The plants are native to the Midwest and Southwest and have spread into adjoining areas.

TOXIC PART: Green fruit.

POISONING: Like all nightshades, the berries contain the glycoalkaloid solanine. The poisonous unripe berries can be attractive to children and curious adults. The ripe berries are not commonly used for pies and jellies like some other nightshades.

SYMPTOMS: Nausea, vomiting, diarrhea, abdominal pain, circulatory and respiratory depression.

COMMENT: Poisonings by these plants are seldom fatal and recovery usually occurs within a few hours to one or two days.

Nutmeg
(Myristica fragrans)

The seeds of nutmeg (mace) contain myristicin, a toxic, yellow volatile oil. Small amounts produce mild hallucinogenic effects; larger amounts produce headache, stomach pain, nausea, vomiting, diarrhea, red skin, dry mouth, double vision, delirium, drowsiness, stupor, sometimes acute panic, unconsciousness, and even death in children. As few as two seeds (nutmegs) can be fatal.

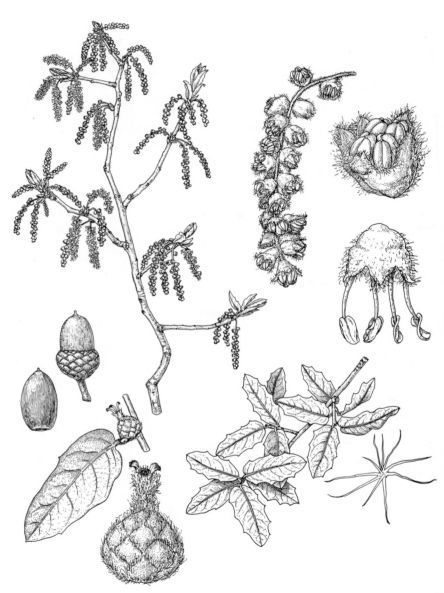

EMORY OAK Note the simple toothed leaves, the drooping male flower clusters and enlarged flowers (upper right), the female flowers (enlarged, lower left), the acorn (enlarged, left center), and star-shaped hair (lower right) of this common southwestern oak.

OAKS

Emory Oak
(Quercus emoryi)

Gambel Oak
(Quercus gambelii) and other species

DESCRIPTION AND DISTRIBUTION: Oaks are deciduous or evergreen shrubs or trees in the beech family that produce acorns — a nut surrounded by a cup at the base. Leaves are simple, alternate, and usually toothed or lobed. Male flowers are in drooping clusters; the separate female flowers are solitary or in clusters. Oaks are widely distributed in the temperate regions of the world and in the tropics at higher elevations.

TOXIC PART: Raw acorns.

POISONING: Oaks have caused extensive loss of livestock due to tannic acid and other unidentified poisonous compounds in the plants and acorns. They are not considered dangerous to humans because only the acorns are eaten and large amounts of the raw acorns are needed to cause poisoning.

SYMPTOMS: Poisonings in livestock result in constipation, bloody stools, and damage to the kidneys.

COMMENT: The ripe acorns are an important source of food for livestock and wildlife and were used extensively for food by Indians and pioneers.

OLEANDER The narrow leathery leaves, the colorful flowers, and the hairy seed and slender seed pod (lower right) are characteristic of this deadly plant.

Oleander

(Nerium oleander)

DESCRIPTION AND DISTRIBUTION: Oleander is a tall shrub of the dogbane family but without milky juice. Leaves are lance-shaped, entire, leathery, and sharp-pointed, appearing opposite or in whorls of three. Flowers are white, pink, or red in showy clusters at the ends of branches. Fruits are long slender capsules, the seeds having a tuft of hairs. Oleanders are native to the Mediterranean and Asiatic regions but are planted as ornamentals in the warmer areas of the world and as potted plants elsewhere.

TOXIC PARTS: Entire plant, especially the leaves.

POISONING: The twigs, green or dry leaves, and flowers contain the extremely poisonous cardiac glycosides oleandrin and nerioside which have physiological action similar to digitalis. A single leaf can kill an adult, and children have been poisoned by chewing the leaves or sucking the nectar from a flower. Severe poisoning may result from using the branches for fuel or as skewers in roasting meat and eating the cooked meat or inhaling the smoke.

SYMPTOMS: Nausea, severe vomiting, stomach pain, bloody diarrhea, dizziness, slowed pulse rate, cold extremities, irregular heartbeat, dilated pupils, drowsiness, unconsciousness, paralysis of lungs, convulsions, coma, and death, usually within a day.

COMMENTS: Honey made from oleander is also poisonous. Contact with the leaves may cause dermatitis in some individuals.

CULTIVATED ONION   The young green onion is shown on the left; the flower and seed stalks in the center; the enlarged flower, fruit, and seed in the upper right; and the onion bulb in the lower right of the drawing of this common food-seasoning plant.

Onion

cultivated onion *(Allium cepa)*

DESCRIPTION AND DISTRIBUTION: Cultivated onions are odoriferous bulbous plants in the amaryllis family (formerly in the lily family). Leaves are basal, long, narrow, and fleshy. Flowers are whitish-green and borne in clusters on leafless, fleshy, round, and hollow flower stalks. Some varieties have bulbs borne in the inflorescences; others bear seeds. Onions are widely cultivated for food and seasoning.

TOXIC PART: Bulbs.

POISONING: Moderate or large amounts of raw or cooked onions in the daily diet of experimental animals for more than a week have produced severe to fatal anemia. Large amounts of culled fresh, rotted, or frozen onions have also killed livestock. The toxic principle is reported to be an alkaloid which may cause anemia in man if consumed in large amounts for similar periods of time. Other persons report severe digestive disturbances from eating small amounts.

SYMPTOMS: Digestive disturbances, anemia, and jaundice. Death may result if onions are eaten in moderate to large amounts for a week or more.

COMMENTS: This valuable food plant shouldn't cause any serious problems as it is usually eaten in moderation. Similarly, wild onions can be used in moderation if properly identified. Other members of this genus are garlic, chives, shallots, and leeks. Onions will flavor the milk of cows grazing them or merely inhaling the fumes.

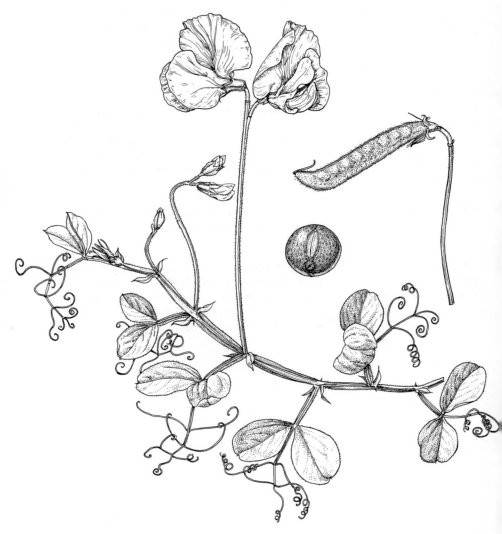

SWEET PEA The conspicuous and colorful butterfly-shaped flower, the pinnately divided leaves with tendrils, and the hairy seed pod and enlarged seed (upper right) characterize this colorful garden forb.

PEAS

Sweet Peas
everlasting peas *(Lathyrus sp.)*

DESCRIPTION AND DISTRIBUTION: Sweet peas are herbaceous annuals or perennials. These sometimes climbing members of the legume family grow worldwide in the temperate zone. Stems are winged or angular. Leaves are pinnately divided, usually with tendrils. Flowers are showy, single or in clusters, and red, pink, white, yellow, blue, or purple in color. Fruit is a usually flat legume pod containing several seeds. Sweet peas are commonly cultivated as ornamentals for their showy flowers. They are distinct from the common English pea *(Pisum sativum)*.

TOXIC PARTS: Entire plant, especially the seeds.

POISONING: Plants contain amine-bearing compounds that cause two types of poisoning. One group of species contains poisons that produce paralysis and skeletal deformities due to disturbed bone formation and excess cartilage growth. The second group of species contain poisons that produce excitement and convulsions. In some countries where the sweet peas were used as food, heavy losses of human life occurred. In this country, losses occur mainly in livestock.

SYMPTOMS: Permanent paralysis, skeletal deformities, slow and weak pulse, shallow breathing, pain, weakness, tremors, excitement, and convulsions. In severe cases death may result.

COMMENTS: Large quantities of sweet pea seeds, raw or cooked, are required to cause poisoning. The wild sweet pea *(Hedysarum mackenzii)* of Alaska and Canada is also reported to be poisonous, so southwestern species of this genus should be suspected.

157

PEACH Note the long, narrow, pointed leaves with saw-toothed edges, the delicate flowers (upper left), and the fleshy fruit, large rough pit, and smooth kernel (lower right) of this valuable fruit tree.

Peach

(Prunus persica, formerly *Amygdalus persica)*

DESCRIPTION AND DISTRIBUTION: Peach is a small cultivated tree in the rose family introduced from China. It has lance-shaped drooping leaves, pink-to-red flowers, and round, juicy, orange yellow fruit with a fuzzy skin and single rough pit. It is cultivated in all temperate climates and is often found as an escape.

TOXIC PARTS: All parts of the plant contain cyanide, especially the seeds, but frosted leaves also have high concentrations.

POISONING: Cyanide is one of the most rapid acting of all poisons. In severe cases death may occur in a few minutes. In other cases symptoms may be delayed until the toxic material is transferred from the acid medium of the stomach to the alkaline medium of the intestine where amygdalin (the naturally occurring compound) is rapidly converted to cyanide. Once absorbed, the hydrocyanic acid paralyzes cell respiration and the victim suffocates for lack of oxygen.

SYMPTOMS: Dizziness, excitement, spasms, and coma. In mild cases, symptoms may include weakness, headache, nausea, vomiting, and irregular heartbeat. In severe cases death may result.

COMMENTS: Most poisonings by cyanide are caused by eating the seeds. Of the cultivated species of *Prunus,* peach seems to be the only one that has caused much trouble in North America. The fleshy part of the peach is edible.

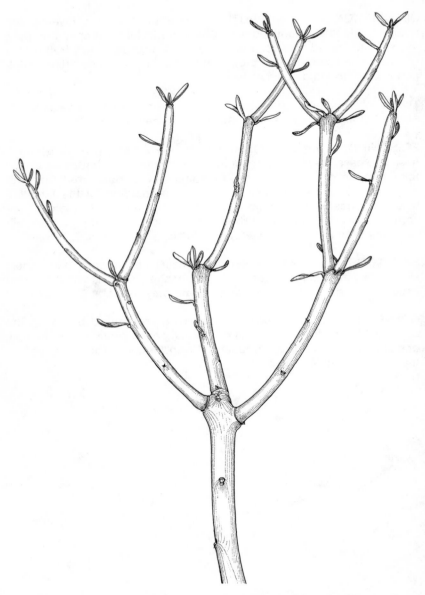

PENCILTREE   Note the succulent, nearly leafless stems and early-deciduous leaves of this odd plant.

Penciltree

milkbush, Indian-tree spurge, malabartree, monkey-fiddle
(Euphorbia tirucalli)

DESCRIPTION AND DISTRIBUTION: Penciltree is a rubbery, spine-less, and usually leafless shrub in the spurge family. The plant has milky juice, and the branches are succulent, green, and round, about the size of a pencil. The small linear leaves are limited to the tips of the branches and soon fall off. Flowers are in clusters at the ends of branches; fruit is a 3-celled capsule. Introduced from Africa, it is widely cultivated as a house and patio plant.

TOXIC PARTS: Leaves, stems, and milky sap.

POISONING: The milky sap contains an irritant that causes dermatitis in some people and can cause severe poisoning when eaten in quantity. However, no cases of fatal poisoning have been documented.

SYMPTOMS: Severe irritation of the mouth, throat, eyes, and stomach; temporary blindness, vomiting, and diarrhea.

COMMENT: Not all plants with milky juice are poisonous. However, because so many plants with milky juice are toxic, it should be considered a signal for caution.

PEPPERS

Chili Pepper

red pepper, cayenne pepper *(Capsicum annuum)*, and other species

Chili peppers are cultivated perennial herbs in the nightshade family native to tropical America. The fruits are grown as a source of chili powder and paprika for use in seasoning, and for medicinal capsicum. The leaves may be cooked and eaten as a vegetable. The plants are also commonly grown as ornamentals.

In contact with the face, eyes, or nostrils, the crushed fruits may cause a burning rash, swollen tissues, and intense eye irritation. If eaten, the fruits cause acute irritation of the lips, mouth, throat, stomach, and intestines which may result in vomiting and diarrhea. A related species, tabasco pepper *(Capsicum frutescens)*, grown commercially for hot sauces, will cause similar but more severe effects. The fruiting plants, peppers, and sauces made from peppers should be kept away from inquisitive children and unwary adults.

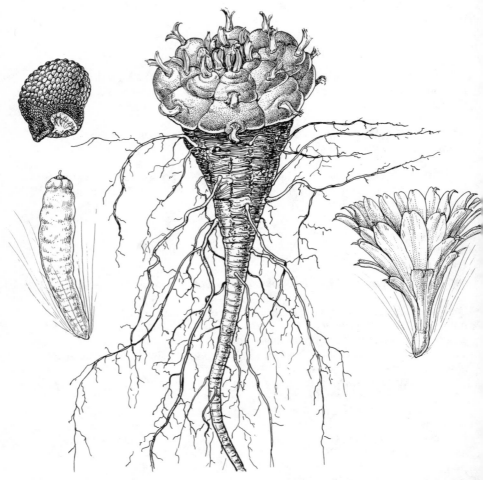

PEYOTE   The cap of buttons on the carrot-like root, the tufts of silky hairs on the buttons, the pink flower (enlarged, lower right), the fruit (enlarged, lower left), and the
seed (enlarged, upper left) characterize this unusual cactus.

Peyote

mescal, mescal buttons *(Lophophora williamsii)*

DESCRIPTION AND DISTRIBUTION: Peyote is a small carrot-shaped, spineless, and fleshy member of the cactus family. Stems are dome-shaped with low rounded knoblike projections (buttons). Flowers are small and bell-shaped, white to rose-pink. Fruit is a pink berry with black seeds. Plants are native to south Texas and northern Mexico and are cultivated elsewhere.

TOXIC PARTS: Entire plant, especially the buttons.

POISONING: The plants contain mescaline, lophophorine, and other alkaloids. Chewing fresh or dried parts of the plant or drinking wine made from the plant have been used by Indians and Mexicans in religious ceremonies to produce hallucinogenic effects.

SYMPTOMS: Vividly colored hallucinations, anxiety, muscular tremors, and twitching. Also: vomiting, diarrhea, stomach pains, pupil dilation, blurred vision, headache, dizziness, illusions, wakefulness, inability to focus one's attention, forgetfulness, loss of sense of time, muscular relaxation, and circulatory depression. Recovery usually occurs within 6 to 8 hours.

COMMENTS: Effects are similar to, but less potent than, those of LSD (lysergic acid diethylamide). Such drugs may be psychologically habit-forming and may cause chromosome damage. Its use is unlawful in some states.

PHILODENDRON   The leaves of these trailing or climbing vines are heart-shaped, vari-
ously colored, and pointed. The leaf of pothos, a similar climbing vine commercially
called philodendron, is shown below.

Philodendrons
(Philodendron sp.)

DESCRIPTION AND DISTRIBUTION: Philodendrons are popular tropical, climbing or erect, ornamental members of the arum family that
sometimes have aerial roots. Leaves are triangular or heart-shaped,
entire to lobed, and vary in color from green to red to white. Leaf blades
can be up to 1.5 m in length. Flowers, when produced, are enclosed in
a leafy bract. Fruit is a white to orange berry. Introduced from tropical
America, they are popular foliage plants for interior decorating and for
landscaping in warmer climates of the world.

TOXIC PARTS: Entire plant.

POISONING: Philodendrons contain calcium oxalate crystals and other
toxins which cause intense burning, swelling, and paralysis of the tissues
when chewed or eaten. The intense burning is due in part to mechanical
injury caused by the sharp crystals and in part to chemical irritation.
Cases of severe poisoning from these plants have not been reported
in the United States.

SYMPTOMS: Burning of the mouth and throat, swelling of the tongue
and throat, choking, salivation, nausea, vomiting, and diarrhea. Symptoms may last for several days or a week or more. Cats have also been
fatally poisoned by eating these plants. Symptoms include debilitation,
listlessness, and loss of kidney function, but no apparent pain.

COMMENTS: There are over 200 species and varieties of *Philodendron*
cultivated as ornamentals. Other members of the arum family grown as
house plants in the Southwest include pothos *(Pothos, Scindapsus* and
Epipremnum sp.*),* windowleaf *(Monstera* sp.*),* spathe flower *(Spathiphyl-
lum* sp.*),* elephant's-ear (see entry), caladium (see entry), and dumbcane
(see entry). Others used as cut flowers in the Southwest include anthurium *(Anthurium* sp.*),* wild calla *(Calla palustris),* and calla lily *(Zantedes-
chia* sp.*).* All have poisonous properties similar to philodendron.

165

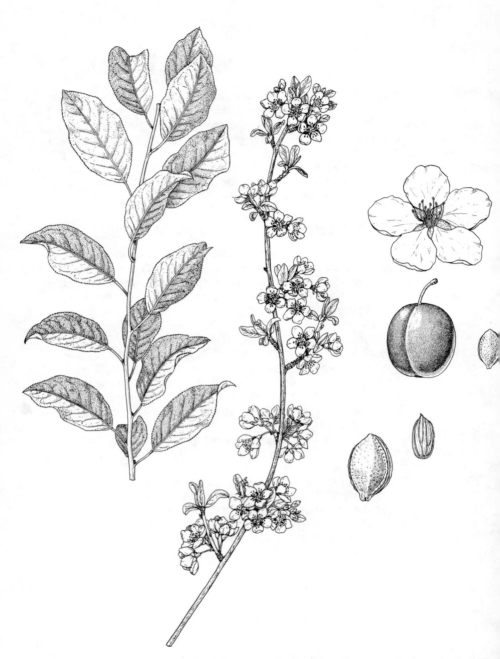

COMMON PLUM The oval saw-toothed leaves, delicate white flowers (enlarged, upper right), medium-sized oval fleshy fruit (right center), and enlarged pit and seed (lower right) are characteristic of this common fruit tree.

PLUMS

Common Plum
(Prunus domestica)

Wild Plum
American plum *(Prunus americana)*

DESCRIPTION AND DISTRIBUTION: Plums are shrubs or small trees of the rose family. Leaves are pointed, oval, and saw-toothed. Flowers are white and solitary or in clusters. Fruit is oval and fleshy with a hard medium-sized pit (seed) and yellow, red, or dark blue plum. The wild plum is native in the forests and mountains; the common plum is from Eurasia. Both are widely cultivated and numerous varieties have been developed.

TOXIC PARTS: Seeds and leaves.

POISONING: The seeds and leaves contain cyanogenic glycosides that hydrolyze into toxic hydrocyanic (prussic) acid. Most cyanide poisonings by plants result from eating the seeds.

SYMPTOMS: Dizziness, spasms, and coma. Also: headache, muscular weakness, nausea, vomiting, difficulty in breathing, and irregular heartbeat.

COMMENTS: The plum is probably the least toxic member of the *Prunus* genus. The fleshy part of the plum is edible.

POINSETTIA The colorful flower clusters are well known to Santa's helpers, but few of them have observed the differences between the female flower (enlarged, lower far left) and male flower (enlarged, lower near left). Note the fruit and seed (upper right) of this popular Christmas shrub.

Poinsettia

common poinsettia, Christmas flower *(Euphorbia pulcherrima,* formerly *Poinsettia pulcherrima)*

DESCRIPTION AND DISTRIBUTION: Poinsettia is a cultivated ornamental shrub in the spurge family, with milky juice. It has large green stem leaves and smaller but showy red, pink, or yellow leaves surrounding the flowers. Fruit is a 3-celled 3-lobed capsule. Introduced from Mexico and South America, it is used extensively as an indoor potted Christmas plant but is also planted outside as an ornamental in the warmer parts of the United States.

TOXIC PARTS: Leaves, stems, and milky sap.

POISONING: Poinsettias contain toxic substances that produce severe gastric distress if eaten. Plants also cause contact dermatitis in susceptible persons.

SYMPTOMS: Severe irritation to the mouth, throat, and stomach; vomiting; diarrhea; and delirium. Blistering of the skin may result from contact with the sap.

COMMENT: Poinsettia has been reported to be fatal to children, but only one questionable case has been documented.

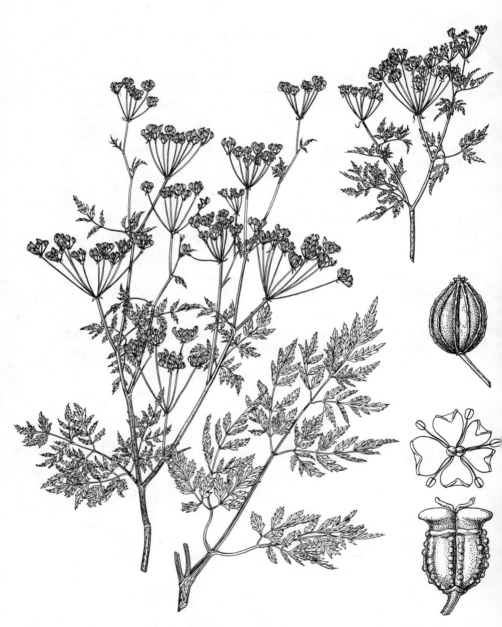

POISON-HEMLOCK   Note the large pinnately divided leaves, the flat-topped clusters of flowers and fruits, the female flower (enlarged, lower right) with enlarged male flower above, and ribbed fruit capsule (enlarged, right center) of this poisonous herb.

Poison-Hemlock

spotted-hemlock, poison-parsley *(Conium maculatum)*

DESCRIPTION AND DISTRIBUTION: Poison-hemlock is a tall biennial forb of the parsley or carrot family with a fleshy taproot and hollow purple-spotted stems. Leaves are clasping, smooth, and pinnately divided 3 to 4 times. Flowers are small and white, in umbrella-shaped clusters. Fruits are dry, ribbed, two-part capsules. Introduced from Eurasia, it is a weed in meadows and along roads and ditchbanks throughout the United States and southern Canada where moisture is adequate.

TOXIC PARTS: Entire plant, especially the seeds and root.

POISONING: The plants contain the intensely poisonous alkaloid coniine and other related alkaloids. Most poisonings occur because the leaves are mistaken for parsley, the roots for parsnips, or the seeds for anise. However, the plant has such an unpleasant taste and odor that toxic quantities are seldom consumed. If not lethal, recovery occurs within a few days.

SYMPTOMS: Burning sensation in mouth and throat, nervousness, trembling, incoordination of body movements, dilation of pupils, muscular weakness, coldness of extremities, weakened and slowed heartbeat, convulsions, and coma. Death occurs through respiratory paralysis.

COMMENTS: Poison-hemlock is believed to be the poison drunk by Socrates. The plant also produces allergenic reactions in sensitive persons.

POISON-IVY   The 3-parted dark green leaves, the flower (enlarged, lower left), the enlarged fruit and cluster of white waxy berries (lower right), and the underground rootstock (bottom) are characteristic of this troublesome shrub.

Poison-Ivy

poison-oak *(Toxicodendron radicans,* formerly *Rhus radicans)*

DESCRIPTION AND DISTRIBUTION: Poison-ivy is a trailing or climbing vine, shrub or small tree in the cashew family. Leaves are 3-foliate with oval, pointed, glossy, and lobed or toothed leaflets. Flowers are greenish-white and clustered in the axils of leaves; fruits are berry-like, whitish, and waxy. This plant is native throughout the Southwest and generally is found in woods and along streams.

TOXIC PARTS: Roots, stems, leaves, pollen, flowers, and fruits.

POISONING: Poison-ivy is not strictly a poisonous plant but rather it is a dermatitis producing plant, since some persons are more affected by it than others due to a pre-existing sensitivity. The skin irritant is an oil-resin containing urushiol. It is in the sap and this is present in all parts of the plant. The irritant is released when the plant is touched or bruised. The irritating chemical is non-volatile but may be spread by other animals or anything touching the plant, such as clothing. Also, it may be carried by pollen or dust particles in the wind or by ashes in smoke. The danger of poisoning is greatest in the spring and summer when plants are full of sap and easily bruised, but dead plants and contaminated clothing, unless cleaned by washing, may remain toxic for years.

SYMPTOMS: The first symptoms are itching, burning, and redness. Small blisters may appear in a few hours or days, depending on the individual's sensitivity. Severe dermatitis characterized by large blisters and swelling of affected parts may remain for several days. Secondary infection may occur due to scratching of affected parts. Severe gastric disturbance and even death may result from eating the leaves or fruits. Also, death may result from severe secondary infection and other complications. Washing with strong soap 5 to 10 minutes after contact will often prevent the symptoms.

COMMENTS: About half of all persons are allergic to poison-ivy. Frequent exposure may increase sensitivity while sensitivity may decrease with lack of exposure. Lacquerware painted with lacquer made from the Asiatic species *(Toxicodendron verniciflua)* can cause dermatitis in susceptible persons. Most shrubby sumacs with long pinnately divided leaves and dense terminal erect flower and fruit clusters are nonpoisonous. Berries of the nontoxic species are relished by wildlife and can be used to make a refreshing beverage. However, they are difficult to distinguish from the toxic varieties, so all sumacs should be avoided.

173

POKEWEED The large, oval, pointed leaves; clusters of flowers (single flower, enlarged, lower left); purplish fruits; and shiny black seed (enlarged, lower left) are characteristic of this attractive, but poisonous, plant.

Pokeweed

pokeberry, skoke, inkweed *(Phytolacca americana)*

DESCRIPTION AND DISTRIBUTION: This shrublike herb with a large fleshy taproot is native to the eastern United States and southeastern Canada. It has been introduced in barnyards and bottomlands in the Chiricahua Mountains and Patagonia hills. Leaves are large, entire, oblong, and pointed. Flowers and fruits are in clusters at the ends of branches. Flowers are white to purplish. Fruit at maturity is a dark purple berry (nearly black) with red juice.

TOXIC PARTS: Entire plant, especially the roots, shoots, and unripe berries.

POISONING: Plants contain the bitter glycoside saponin and a glycoprotein. All parts of the plant are poisonous, but the succulent young shoots can be used as potherbs if cooked in two waters and the waters discarded. The ripe berries when cooked are the least toxic and can be used to make pies. However, the fresh berries are very dangerous to children.

SYMPTOMS: Burning and bitter taste in the mouth, severe stomach cramps and pain, nausea, persistent vomiting, diarrhea, blurred vision, drowsiness, slowed respiration, salivation, perspiration, difficult breathing, weakness, tremors, severe convulsions, spasms, coma, and death (if the plant is eaten in large amounts).

COMMENTS: This plant is very dangerous if the leaves are eaten without proper cooking or if the roots are pulled up with the leaves. Birds eat the berries without harm. The root was used as a source of medicine by Indians and early settlers, and overdoses resulted in many poisonings.

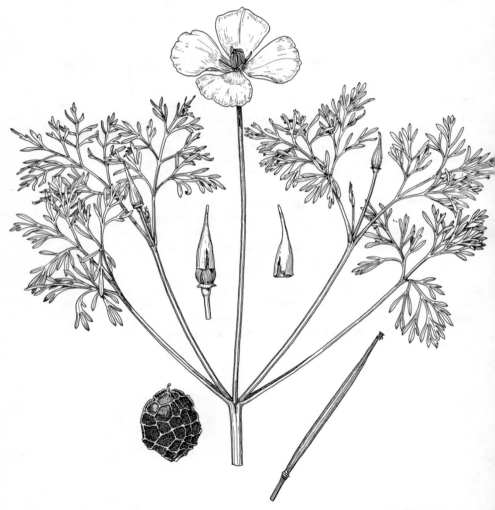

GOLD POPPY The beautiful gold or yellow flower, the dissected leaves, the splitting
cap slipping off the bud (center), the slender seed capsule (lower right), and the pitted
seed (enlarged, lower left) characterize this attractive desert forb.

POPPIES

Gold Poppy
Mexican gold poppy *(Eschscholtzia mexicana)* and other species

DESCRIPTION AND DISTRIBUTION: Gold poppy is closely related to California poppy *(Eschscholtzia californica).* They are annual and perennial herbs in the poppy family native to the Southwest. Plants have smooth whitish stems and leaves. Leaves are dissected into narrow lobes. Flowers are poppy-like and deep orange to pale yellow.

TOXIC PART: Juice of the fruits.

POISONING: The colorless juice is reported to be mildly narcotic and was used by the Indians to relieve toothache.

SYMPTOMS: Mildly narcotic.

COMMENTS: Even though these species are members of a poisonous family, there is no evidence that they cause serious poisonings. In the spring in favorable years they cover the landscape with showy orange-colored flowers.

OPIUM POPPY Large and colorful flowers, clasping toothed leaves, the distinctive crowned capsule, and the checkered seed (enlarged, upper left) are characteristic of this attractive herb.

POPPIES

Opium Poppy
common poppy *(Papaver somniferum)*

DESCRIPTION AND DISTRIBUTION: Opium poppy is an erect annual herb of the poppy family with a white "bloom" on the foliage. The plant has milky juice. Leaves are simple and coarsely toothed or lobed, with clasping upper leaves. Flowers are solitary at the ends of long stalks and have showy red, white, pink, or purple petals that are sometimes fringed. The fruit is an oval crowned capsule filled with tiny poppy seeds. This species was introduced from Eurasia and was widely grown in the United States for its colorful flowers until its cultivation without a license became unlawful.

TOXIC PARTS: Unripe fruits or their juice.

POISONING: The crude resin obtained by cutting the unripe seed capsules is the source of narcotic opium alkaloids. This is also the source of such medicinally valuable (or harmful, if misused) alkaloids as morphine, codeine, and papaverine which are used to relieve pain.

SYMPTOMS: Eating the unripe fruit or its juice produces sleepiness, stupor, coma, shallow and slow breathing, and profound depression of the central nervous system. It may also produce nausea and severe retching and is habit forming. Overdoses may cause death due to respiratory failure.

COMMENTS: The opium poppy seeds used as topping on breads have only minute traces of alkaloids and are harmless. The seeds are also used for seasoning food and as a source of edible oil. Other species of *Papaver,* such as oriental poppy *(Papaver orientale),* are not toxic.

PRICKLE POPPY   The large usually white attractive flowers; the densely prickly stems, leaves, and seed pods (enlarged seed pod, upper right); and the pitted seed (enlarged, right center) characterize this pretty but untouchable forb.

POPPIES

Prickle Poppy

prickly poppy, thornapple *(Argemone platyceras),* and other species

DESCRIPTION AND DISTRIBUTION: Prickle poppies are erect perennial herbs of the poppy family with bitter yellow or orange sap. Plants are densely covered with short yellow spines. Leaves are clasping and pinnately cleft with spine-tipped lobes. Flowers are large and showy with white, yellow, or lavender petals. Fruit is a usually prickly capsule with many small seeds. Various species are native to North and South America.

TOXIC PARTS: Seeds and expressed oil.

POISONING: Leaves and seeds contain the toxic alkaloids protopine, berberine, sanguinarine, and dihydrosanguinarine. Poisoning occurs when grains, such as corn, oats, or wheat, become contaminated with prickle poppy seeds, or people experiment with the plant.

SYMPTOMS: Vomiting, diarrhea, visual disturbances, distention of the abdomen, fainting, and coma. Victims usually recover without serious consequences.

COMMENT: The acrid yellow juice of Mexican prickle poppy *(Argemone mexicana)* has been used to treat skin diseases.

POTATO   The pinnately divided leaves, the white or bluish flower (upper left), the yellowish or green berries (lower right), and sprouted tuber (lower left) are characteristic of this important, sometimes poisonous, food plant.

Potato

Irish potato, white potato *(Solanum tuberosum)*

DESCRIPTION AND DISTRIBUTION: Potatoes are upright herbs of the nightshade family with edible underground tubers (swollen underground stems) containing starch and other reserve food material. Leaves are oval and pinnately divided. Flowers are white or bluish and borne in clusters. Fruits are rounded yellowish or green berries. The plant is believed native to the Andes in South America and is widely cultivated in temperate regions as one of the world's most important food plants.

TOXIC PARTS: Green and spoiled potatoes, sprouts, and unripe berries.

POISONING: Potatoes contain the glycoalkaloid solanine which is highly toxic. It is concentrated under the skin in spoiled and sunburned spots, and in sprouts. Sprouts should be removed and green or sunburned potatoes peeled before cooking. Spoiled potatoes should be discarded.

SYMPTOMS: Nausea, vomiting, diarrhea, headache, stomach pain, cold and clammy skin, dilated pupils, circulatory and respiratory depression, shock, and paralysis. In severe cases, death may result.

COMMENTS: Death is uncommon because sprouted potatoes are usually peeled, and boiling potatoes tends to leach out the solanine into the cooking water where it is diluted and partially destroyed. The skin of baked potatoes is harmless when eaten in normal quantities.

JAPANESE PRIVET Note the lance-shaped leaves, the dense flower clusters, the flower (enlarged, upper right), the fruiting branch, and the smooth berry and rough seed (both enlarged, lower center) of this ornamental hedge, shrub, or tree.

PRIVETS

Japanese Privet

waxleaf privet *(Ligustrum japonicum)* and other species

DESCRIPTION AND DISTRIBUTION: Japanese privet is an evergreen shrub of the olive family introduced from Asia. Leaves are simple and entire, opposite, long and smooth, pointed, and leathery. Flowers are small white and tubular, borne in terminal clusters. Fruits are blue or black and berry-like. Japanese privet is cultivated as a hedge throughout the warmer sections of the South and Southwest. Other species are planted throughout the United States and Canada.

TOXIC PARTS: Berries and leaves.

POISONING: Privets contain poisonous alkaloids, and children have been fatally poisoned by eating the berries. The leaves are also poisonous to livestock and should be considered dangerous.

SYMPTOMS: Nausea, vomiting, diarrhea, subnormal temperature, muscular twitching, kidney damage, convulsions, and paralysis. In severe cases, death may result.

COMMENTS: Although few cases of poisoning have been reported in this country, privet should be treated with caution and berries kept away from children. Birds rarely eat the berries.

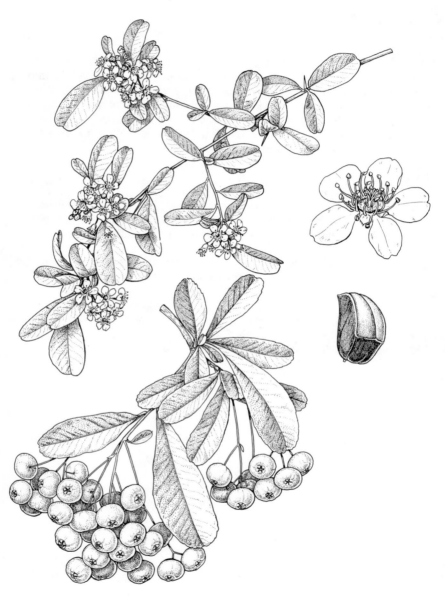

PYRACANTHA   The paddle-shaped leaves, the white flowers (enlarged, upper right), the abundant berries, and seed (enlarged, right center) are characteristic of this attractive ornamental shrub.

Pyracantha

firethorn *(Pyracantha* sp.*)*

DESCRIPTION AND DISTRIBUTION: Pyracantha is an evergreen, usually thorny shrub in the rose family. Leaves are oblong and shiny with
wavy or toothed margins. Flowers are white in dense clusters. The small
red or orange berry-like fruits are persistent and showy in the winter.
The plants are widely planted in mild climates as ornamentals and
hedges and are often espaliered.

TOXIC PART: Berries are suspected.

POISONING: Berries have been suspected of being poisonous, but
studies have shown that the berries themselves are harmless, at least
in the quantities likely to be eaten. However, pesticide sprays used to
control red spider may make them toxic to birds and children.

SYMPTOMS: Unknown.

COMMENTS: The colorful berries are very attractive to children but
they have an unpleasant taste. Jelly may be made from the berries.

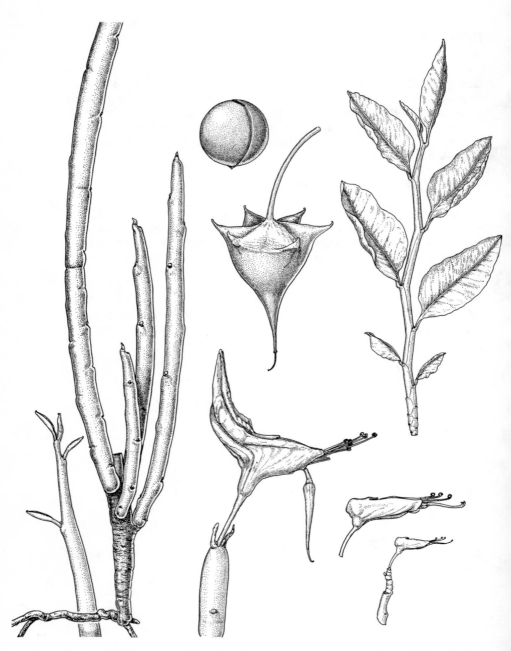

REDBIRD-CACTUSES The fleshy stems; minute early-deciduous leaves; unique flower, distinctive seed, and seed pod (enlarged, center) of *Pedilanthus macrocarpus* are shown on the left; the larger leaves and flowers of *Pedilanthus tithymaloides* are on the right.

Redbird-Cactuses

slipperflowers *(Pedilanthus macrocarpus* and *tithymaloides)*

DESCRIPTION AND DISTRIBUTION: These plants are odd looking succulent shrubs of the spurge family with milky juice. Leaves are minute to large and deciduous to persistent. Flowers are red to purple and shaped like birds or slippers. Fruit is a 3-celled capsule. These plants are introduced from drier sites in tropical America and grown as ornamentals in warm climates.

TOXIC PARTS: All parts.

POISONING: The leaves, stems, flowers, or seeds, if eaten in quantity, can cause severe poisoning. The sap can cause dermatitis in sensitive persons and painful irritation or injury to the eyes and skin.

SYMPTOMS: Dermatitis, nausea, vomiting, stomach pain, and diarrhea.

COMMENTS: These plants can cause severe dermatitis, stomach, and intestinal problems in young children and should be kept out of their reach.

RHODODENDRON and **AZALEA** Colorful flowers and attractive leaves characterize these beautiful ornamental shrubs.

Rhododendrons, Azaleas
(Rhododendron sp.)

DESCRIPTION AND DISTRIBUTION: Rhododendrons and azaleas are usually evergreen shrubs belonging to the heath family. Leaves are simple, leathery, mostly entire, and alternate or in whorls. Flowers are white-to-pink and showy, usually borne in terminal clusters. Fruit is a woody capsule. They occur throughout the temperate parts of the world and the United States as native and introduced ornamental plants.

TOXIC PARTS: Entire plant.

POISONING: Plants contain the resinoid carbohydrate andromedotoxin. The leaves, twigs, flowers, and pollen grains contain the resinoid. Children have been poisoned by sucking the flowers or making tea from the leaves, but cases of poisoning are rare. Symptoms appear about 6 hours after ingestion.

SYMPTOMS: Watering of the mouth and eyes, nasal discharge, nausea, severe abdominal pain, vomiting, convulsions, slow pulse, lowered blood pressure, lack of coordination, and loss of energy. In severe cases there is progressive paralysis of the arms and legs until death.

COMMENTS: Honey made from the flowers may be poisonous, but it is so bitter that poisonous amounts will rarely be eaten. Cemetery wreaths and stage decorations made from the plants have caused deaths in other animals.

RHUBARB   Note the large fan-shaped leaf blade and fleshy leaf stalk of this excellent pie plant. The flowers and seeds are rarely produced.

Rhubarb

garden rhubarb, pieplant, wineplant *(Rheum rhabarbarum,*
formerly *Rheum rhaponticum)*

DESCRIPTION AND DISTRIBUTION: Rhubarb is a garden vegetable in
the buckwheat family introduced from Asia and grown for its thick fleshy
leaf stalks (petioles) which make excellent pies, preserves, and sauces.
It has large radial leaves growing 25 to 50 cm tall from thick rootstocks.
The small greenish, white, or reddish flowers, when produced, are borne
in narrow clusters on long stalks. Fruit is a small winged seed. The plant
is cultivated throughout the cooler regions of the world.

TOXIC PARTS: Leaf blades.

POISONING: The leaf blades contain oxalic acid and soluble oxalates
of potassium and calcium. Ingestion of raw or cooked leaf blades may
cause severe irritation and corrosion of the mouth, stomach, and intestines resulting in diarrhea with bloody stools. Precipitation of insoluble
calcium oxalate crystals can cause muscle and kidney damage and block
urination. The leaves also can cause dermatitis.

SYMPTOMS: Nausea, violent vomiting, nasal bleeding, stomach pains,
headache, backache, weakness, difficulty in breathing, burning of mouth
and throat, kidney failure, internal bleeding from non-coagulation of
blood, and coma. Death occurs rapidly if large amounts of leaf blades
are eaten.

COMMENTS: The leaf stalks do not contain oxalic acid or soluble
oxalates and are safe to eat. The leaf stalks do contain harmless malic
and citric acids which give rhubarb its deliciously tart flavor. Death
rarely occurs because of the known toxicity of the blades.

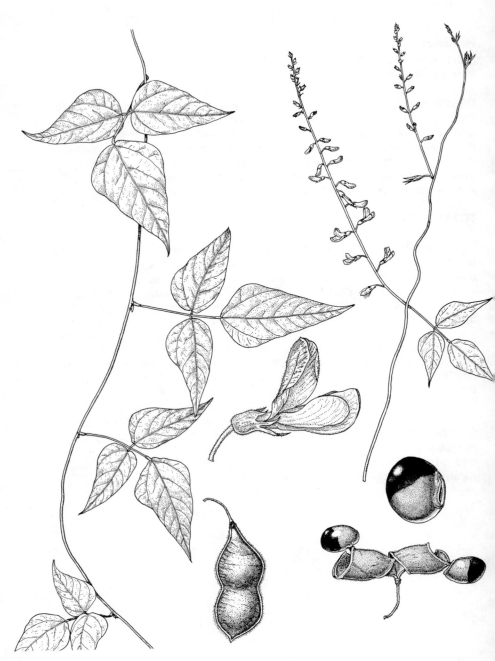

ROSARY BEAN   The twining stem, the 3-foliate leaves, the legume flowers, the hairy
seed pod, and the attractive red and black beans characterize this unusual plant.

ROSARY BEANS

Precatory Bean
rosary pea, jequirity bean, crabseye, prayer bean, love bean, lucky bean
(Abrus precatorius)

DESCRIPTION AND DISTRIBUTION: Precatory bean is a twining, more or less woody perennial vine of the legume family. Leaves are alternate and pinnately divided into many small leaflets. Flowers are rose to purple, rarely white, small and pea-like growing in axillary clusters. Fruit is a short legume pod. Seeds are oval, brilliant red and jet black shiny beans. Native to the tropics, precatory bean is naturalized in Florida. However, the beans are made into rosaries, necklaces, bracelets, leis, and various toys which are distributed nationwide.

TOXIC PART: Seeds.

POISONING: These attractive beans are favorite playthings for children. They contain the phytotoxin abrin, one of the most toxic natural substances, and the tetanic glycoside abric acid. Poisoning results when the seeds are chewed and swallowed. Whole seeds are impermeable and, if swallowed, pass through the intestinal tract. It is reported that one seed thoroughly chewed is enough to kill a child or an adult. Sometimes symptoms do not appear until 1 to 3 days after ingestion.

SYMPTOMS: Severe stomach pain, nausea, vomiting, diarrhea, trembling, weakness, cold sweat, drowsiness, labored breathing, anemia, convulsions, weak and fast pulse, kidney failure, circulatory collapse, coma, and death.

COMMENTS: Poisoning can result from pricking a finger while stringing the beads. The soft, immature beans can be chewed easily and are always a hazard. Obviously, necklaces and other beans should be kept out of reach of small children and curious adults.

Rosary Beans
piule *(Rhynchosia* sp.*)*

Rosary bean plants are weak and twining, native and exotic, perennial herbs distinguished from precatory bean plants by having only 3 leaflets. They have similar red and black seeds that have hallucinogenic and other poisonous properties. The seeds of some species are important in folk medicine in several countries.

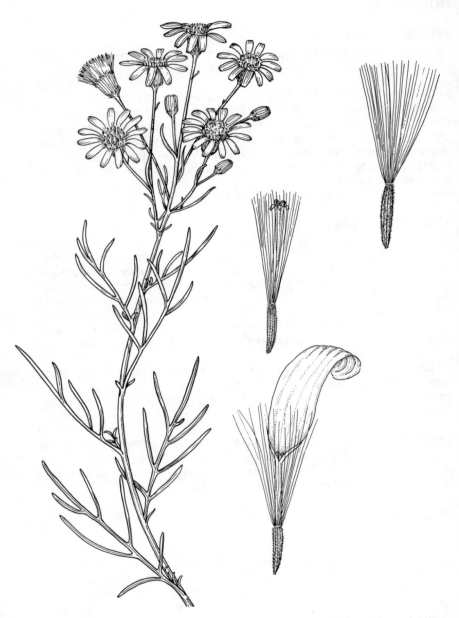

THREADLEAF GROUNDSEL White wooly stems, showy yellow flowers (enlarged disc and ray flowers, center and lower right), pinnately lobed leaves, and achene fruit (upper right) characterize this unusual shrub.

SENECIOS

Threadleaf Groundsel
(Senecio douglasii var. *longilobus)* and other species

DESCRIPTION AND DISTRIBUTION: Threadleaf groundsel is a shrub in the sunflower family. Stems are covered with a white wool. Most leaves are pinnately divided into long slender lobes. Flowers are in yellow heads scattered throughout the plant. The seed is enclosed in a dry pod which has a pappus of whitish capillary bristles. The plant is common throughout the Southwest, growing in dry plains and washes and flowering throughout most of the year.

TOXIC PARTS: Entire plant.

POISONING: The toxins are pyrrolizidine alkaloids that cause liver injury. The alkaloids cause functional death of the liver cells and rupture the veins that supply blood to the liver. This may occur rapidly or over a period of time. Death results when the liver deteriorates to the point that it can no longer sustain its vital processes. Death of humans in undeveloped countries has resulted from eating bread contaminated with seeds or leaves of senecio, and from drinking a supposedly medicinal tea made from the plant. The recent use of native plants in the United States has resulted in irreparable liver damage and death for individuals drinking gordolobo tea mistakenly made from threadleaf groundsel.

SYMPTOMS: Nervousness, nausea, vomiting, diarrhea, loss of appetite and weight, weakness, abdominal pain, jaundice, and death.

COMMENTS: Not all senecios are poisonous. Some plants may also cause dermatitis. Another group of native and introduced plants, the crotalarias *(Crotalaria* sp.*),* are legumes that contain similar alkaloids and cause similar liver damage. The alkaloids are not destroyed by drying.

HEMP SESBANIA Note the long, pinnately divided leaflets, the pea-shaped flowers, and the long slender pod and rectangular plump seed (enlarged, lower left) of this unusual legume.

SESBANIAS

Hemp Sesbania

Colorado River hemp *(Sesbania exaltata,* formerly
Sesbania macrocarpa) and other species

DESCRIPTION AND DISTRIBUTION: Hemp sesbania is a tall annual,
sometimes shrubby, member of the legume family. Leaves are long and
pinnately divided, with up to 35 pairs of leaflets. Flowers are yellow,
often purple spotted, and pea-shaped in loose axillary clusters. Pods
are long and slender, up to 20 cm long, and tipped with a slender beak.
Seeds are rectangular, plump, and dark brown. Hemp sesbania is native
to the South and Southwest, growing in moist ground and along streams.
It has been grown as a green manure or cover crop and is a weed in old
fields and along roadsides.

TOXIC PARTS: Seeds and flowers.

POISONING: The seeds and flowers contain saponins that may cause
poisoning if eaten. Leaves are less toxic. Symptoms may not develop
until 1 to 2 days after eating.

SYMPTOMS: Depression, nausea, repeated vomiting, abdominal pain,
diarrhea, and rapid pulse. In severe cases there can be weakness, difficult breathing, and death.

COMMENTS: Hemp sesbania is a fiber plant used by the Yuma Indians
to make thread for fish nets and fish lines. The seeds are eaten by birds,
apparently without harm. Other poisonous sesbanias, native and introduced, are found in the Southeast and along the Pacific coast.

SNOW-ON-THE-MOUNTAIN Note the attractive, white-margined leaves and flower clusters of this striking plant. An enlarged flower is shown at the lower right, a developing ovary at the upper right, and an enlarged mature fruit and seed at upper left.

Snow-on-the-Mountain

(Euphorbia marginata)

DESCRIPTION AND DISTRIBUTION: Snow-on-the-mountain is a tall annual herb in the spurge family with milky juice, growing up to 1 m in height. Leaves are lance-shaped and smooth, bordered by conspicuously white margins. Flowers are bordered with a whorl of white petal-like leaves. Fruit is a 3-celled 3-lobed capsule. Snow-on-the-mountain is native to the western part of the United States from Canada to Mexico. It is commonly planted in gardens and has escaped widely in the eastern United States.

TOXIC PARTS: Leaves, stems, and milky sap.

POISONING: Snow-on-the-mountain contains toxins that cause dermatitis, severe irritation to the digestive tract, and can be fatal. In one case, the use of a concoction from snow-on-the-mountain in an effort to induce abortion resulted in the death of the young woman. It is also suspected of poisoning honey and can produce undesirable flavors in milk.

SYMPTOMS: Symptoms include blistering of the skin; severe irritation of the mouth, throat, and stomach; nausea; abdominal pain; fainting; and diarrhea. In severe cases death may result.

COMMENTS: The milky juice of this spurge is so caustic that it has been used instead of a hot iron to brand cattle. Another native species, white-margined spurge or rattlesnake weed *(Euphorbia albomarginata),* was used by the Pima Indians as an emetic and to treat snakebite.

SOAPBERRY   Note the long, pinnately divided leaves, the large flower clusters, the flower (enlarged, lower right), the wrinkled fruits (enlarged, upper right), and seed (enlarged, right center) of this distinctive southwestern shrub or small tree.

Soapberry

western soapberry, wild chinaberry *(Sapindus drummondii)*

DESCRIPTION AND DISTRIBUTION: Soapberry is a large shrub or small tree in the soapberry family. Leaves are large and pinnately divided into 8 to 18 pointed, linear, entire leaflets. Flowers are small and whitish, in clusters at the ends of branches. Fruit is berry-like and yellow. The species is native to the southwestern United States and northern Mexico.

TOXIC PART: Fruits.

POISONING: The plants, especially the fruits, contain poisonous saponins, one of which is a digitalis extract. Poisoning of humans is apparently rare but the berries should be regarded with caution. The berries also cause dermatitis.

SYMPTOMS: Symptoms are undocumented but upset stomach and visual disturbances can be expected.

COMMENTS: The crushed fruits have been used in Mexico to stupefy fish and as a laundry soap. The fruit is also used medicinally as a remedy for kidney disorders, rheumatism, and fevers. Also, buttons and necklaces are made from the seeds.

SPINACH The basal rosette of spinach is shown in the center, the female flower (enlarged) and arrangement in the upper right, the male flower (enlarged) and arrangement in the lower right, and the seed (enlarged) in the lower left.

Spinach
(Spinacea oleracea)

DESCRIPTION AND DISTRIBUTION: Spinach is an erect annual herb of the goosefoot family introduced from Asia. The basal leaves are oval, lobed at the base, and grow in a rosette. Stem leaves are narrower and become progressively smaller towards the apex. The small male flowers grow in elongated terminal clusters, the female flowers in the leaf axils, each on separate plants. Seeds are enclosed in a small bladder. Plants are widely cultivated for salads and as a potherb.

TOXIC PART: Leaves.

POISONING: Spinach contains over 10% soluble salts of oxalic acid that can combine with calcium to form an insoluble calcium oxalate which precipitates in the intestinal tract and is excreted. As a result, regular consumption of moderate to large amounts of spinach combined with a low calcium diet can create a calcium deficiency, a condition which has caused death of laboratory animals. Large concentrations of oxalates in the bloodstream may also result in the precipitation of oxalate crystals in the kidneys, plugging the kidney tubules and urinary tract. Another toxic substance in spinach is nitrate, which is reported to have caused nitrate poisoning of infants in France and Germany. However, occasional consumption of spinach will rarely cause ill effects. Spinach is also reported to cause diarrhea in infants.

SYMPTOMS: Diarrhea and possible calcium deficiency, resulting in convulsions and collapse. In severe cases death may result.

COMMENTS: Other common potherbs containing high levels of oxalic acid are beet tops *(Beta vulgaris)*, Swiss chard *(Beta vulgaris* var. *cicla)*, and New Zealand spinach *(Tetragonia expansa)*. Wild plants sometimes used as pot herbs that contain high levels of oxalic acid include purslane *(Portulaca oleracea)*, lambsquarter *(Chenopodium album)*, and pokeweed *(Phytolacca americana)*. Oxalate content in these plants is highest in the late summer and fall and may be as high as 35% of the plant.

STAR-OF-BETHLEHEM The showy white flowers, long narrow leaves, and bulbs are characteristic of these poisonous lilies.

SQUILL

Red Squill
(Urginea maritima)

The bulb of this lily, introduced from the Mediterranean region, is used to make the rat poison, red squill. The bulbs and the rat poison are distasteful to humans and are quickly vomited up, so they present little danger to man. Species of the closely related genus *Scilla* are also called squill. They are occasionally grown as ornamentals in greenhouses and outdoors in mild regions. Several species are toxic, and bulbs should be kept out of reach of children.

Star-of-Bethlehem
(Ornithogalum sp.)

DESCRIPTION AND DISTRIBUTION: These onion-like members of the lily family were introduced from the Mediterranean region. The erect and linear basal leaves form a clump and have a light green midrib. The white, showy, star-like flowers are borne in clusters on a leafless stalk. The fruit is a 3-lobed, several-seeded capsule. Various species are naturalized in the central and eastern United States and are grown as ornamentals elsewhere.

TOXIC PARTS: Bulbs, leaves, and flowers, both fresh and dried.

POISONING: The plants contain several poisonous alkaloids. Children have been poisoned by eating the flowers and bulbs of this attractive plant.

SYMPTOMS: Nausea, vomiting, diarrhea, and stomach pain. In severe cases death may result.

COMMENTS: Because the flowers of some species persist several weeks without water, they are used as cut flowers in arrangements. Care should be taken to keep these flowers away from children.

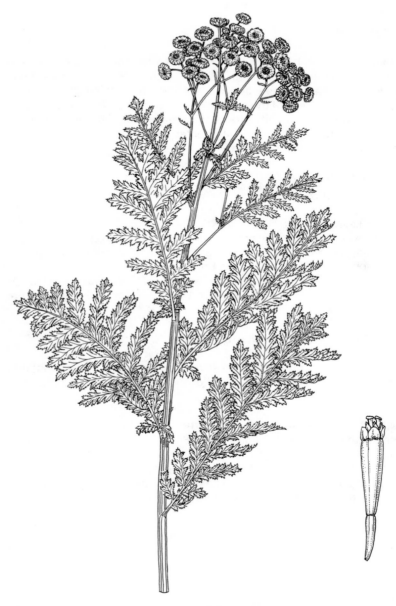

TANSY The yellow flower clusters, the pinnately divided leaves, and the tubular flower (enlarged, lower right) characterize this ancient herbal and medicinal plant.

Tansy

common tansy *(Tanacetum vulgare)*

DESCRIPTION AND DISTRIBUTION: Common tansy is a tall, aromatic, perennial herb in the sunflower family growing from a rootstock. Leaves are pinnately divided into toothed or lobed leaflets. Flowers are enclosed in yellow heads, one-to-several on each flower stalk. Fruit is a dry, one-seeded, 5-ribbed capsule with a minute crown. Introduced from Eurasia it is widely naturalized in North America, being grown as an ornamental and for medicinal purposes.

TOXIC PARTS: Leaves, stems, and flowers.

POISONING: The leaves and stems are used to produce tanacetin, the oil of tansy used as a home remedy for nervousness, to kill intestinal worms, to promote menstruation, and to induce abortion. Humans have been poisoned by taking overdoses of the oil or by drinking tea made from the leaves and flowers.

SYMPTOMS: Skin irritation, nausea, vomiting, diarrhea, convulsions, frothing at the mouth, violent spasms, dilated pupils, frequent and feeble pulse, kidney damage, and sometimes death.

COMMENT: Tansy produces undesirable flavors in the milk of cows, but the plants are rarely eaten by cows because of their bitter taste.

TREE and DESERT TOBACCOS The large oval leaves of tree tobacco **are shown** above, the flowers in the center, and the seed (enlarged) in the right center. The flowers, leaves, seed (enlarged), and seed pods of desert tobacco are at lower left.

TOBACCOS

Tree Tobacco
(Nicotiana glauca) and other species

DESCRIPTION AND DISTRIBUTION: Tree tobacco is a shrub or small tree in the nightshade family with a whitish smooth bark. The entire oval leaves are thick and rubbery. The yellow flowers are tubular and borne in dense or loose clusters at the ends of branches. The fruit is a many-seeded capsule. Tree tobacco is introduced from South America and is widely naturalized in the southeastern and southwestern United States.

TOXIC PARTS: Entire plant.

POISONING: The plants contain nicotine and other alkaloids which are extremely poisonous. Poisoning has resulted from persons using the raw leaves for salad, the boiled leaves for greens, or sucking the flowers.

SYMPTOMS: Symptoms vary with dosage. They include nausea, burning of mouth and intestinal tract, severe vomiting, diarrhea, stomach pains, slow pulse, muscular weakness, cold sweat, irregular heartbeat, depression, dizziness, convulsions, respiratory failure, paralysis, and prostration. Occasionally poisoning is fatal. Death may occur within a few minutes or several days.

COMMENTS: Native southwestern species, such as desert tobacco *(Nicotiana trigonophylla),* may be equally dangerous. Use of nicotine as an insecticide should be made with caution as toxic doses can be readily absorbed through the skin.

TOMATO   The large pinnately divided and lobed leaves, the drooping yellow flowers (enlarged, right center), and the fruit and enlarged seed (lower right) characterize this important garden vegetable.

Tomato
loveapple *(Lycopersicon lycopersicum)*

DESCRIPTION AND DISTRIBUTION: Tomato is an erect to trailing, often hairy, unarmed herb of the nightshade family introduced from South America. Leaves are pinnately divided or lobed and toothed. Flowers are yellow, deeply 5-lobed, and borne in loose clusters. Fruit is a smooth and more or less round, usually red (sometimes yellow or orange) small to large pulpy berry. Tomato is widely cultivated as a food crop in the temperate regions.

TOXIC PARTS: Leaves, vines, and sprouts.

POISONING: Tomato contains the violently toxic alkaloid solanine, found principally in the vines, but the green fruits may also contain toxic quantities. Poisonings have resulted from drinking tea made from the leaves.

SYMPTOMS: Headache, stomach pain, vomiting, diarrhea, subnormal temperature, and circulatory and respiratory depression.

COMMENTS: Grafting of tomato shoots on roots of the closely related jimsonweed in an effort to produce larger, more cold-resistant tomatoes, resulted in the production of fruits that caused severe poisoning when eaten raw. The plants have also been known to produce dermatitis in susceptible persons.

VIRGINIA CREEPER The large, palmately divided leaves, the flower (enlarged, left center), the blue-black berry and seed (enlarged, lower left), and the tendrils (upper right) characterize this climbing woody vine.

Virginia Creeper

woodbine, American ivy *(Parthenocissus quinquefolia)*

DESCRIPTION AND DISTRIBUTION: Virginia creeper is a high-climbing woody vine of the grape family native to temperate Asia and North America. The vines attach themselves with tendrils which often have disc-like tips. Leaves are palmately divided into five lance-shaped toothed leaflets. Flowers are small and greenish, growing in clusters at the tips of branches. Fruit is a black or blue black berry. This plant is widely cultivated as an ornamental and grows on walls, fences, and trees. Its attractive green leaves turn a brilliant red in the fall.

TOXIC PARTS: Berries and probably leaves.

POISONING: The small blue berries are attractive to children and have been suspected of causing poisoning and death of children in a number of cases. The toxic principle is oxalic acid.

SYMPTOMS: Nausea, abdominal pain, vomiting, diarrhea (sometimes bloody), headache, drowsiness, stupor, muscle cramps, twitching of facial muscles, and kidney failure. In severe cases death may result.

COMMENTS: Children should be cautioned not to eat the berries. The bark has been used medicinally.

DOUGLAS WATERHEMLOCK   Note the large, pinnately divided leaves, the umbrella-shaped flower and seed clusters, the interesting flower (enlarged, lower right), the ribbed seed capsule (enlarged, left center), and the chambered rootstock with attached tubers (lower left) of this dangerous plant.

WATERHEMLOCKS

Douglas Waterhemlock
(Cicuta douglasii) and other species

DESCRIPTION AND DISTRIBUTION: Waterhemlocks are tall, native perennial herbs of the parsley or carrot family with hollow stems and a bundle of short rootstocks. The roots have hollow horizontal chambers that exude a gummy and oily yellow juice when cut. Leaves are clasping, alternate, and pinnately divided 2 to 3 times into narrow toothed and pointed leaflets, with the secondary veins ending in the notches. Flowers are small and white in terminal flat-topped clusters. Fruits are dry, ribbed, two-part capsules. Various species are found throughout North America along streams and in wet meadows.

TOXIC PARTS: Entire plant, especially the roots and young growth.

POISONING: The toxin is the resin-like higher alcohol cicutoxin that acts on the central nervous system. The root is extremely poisonous and one mouthful is sufficient to kill a man. Children have been poisoned by making whistles and peashooters from the hollow stems. Most poisonings result when waterhemlocks are mistaken for wild artichoke or parsnip.

SYMPTOMS: Frothing at the mouth, tremors, spasms, dilated pupils, extreme stomach pain, diarrhea, violent convulsions, vomiting, delirium, respiratory failure, paralysis, and death. Symptoms usually appear within a half hour after consumption of a lethal dose.

COMMENTS: These plants are considered by many to be the most violently poisonous plants in the North Temperate Zone. Douglas waterhemlock is the most common southwestern waterhemlock.

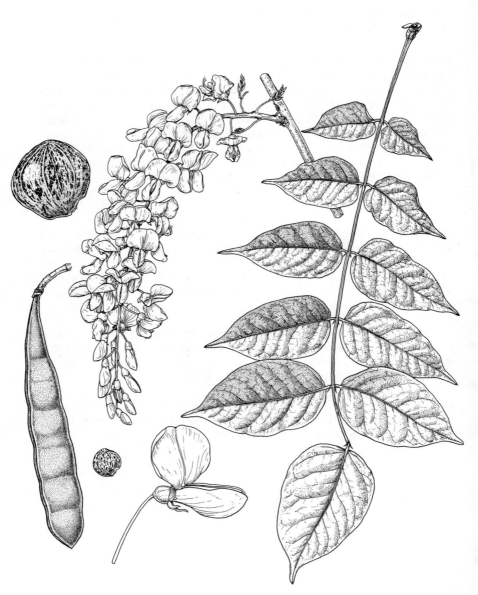

JAPANESE WISTERIA The large, pinnately divided leaf, the pendulous cluster of colorful flowers (single flower shown enlarged, lower center), and the seed pod and seed (enlarged, upper left) characterize this attractive woody vine.

WISTERIAS

Japanese Wisteria
(Wisteria floribunda)

Chinese Wisteria
(Wisteria sinensis)

DESCRIPTION AND DISTRIBUTION: Wisterias are twining woody vines in the legume family native to temperate eastern Asia. Leaves are large, alternate, and pinnately compound. Flowers are pea-shaped and white, bluish, purplish, red, or pink, being borne in large, showy, pendulous clusters. Fruit is a long, thick, flat, knobby legume pod. These plants are widely cultivated as ornamentals in the temperate regions of the United States and have escaped in the southeastern states.

TOXIC PARTS: Pods and seeds.

POISONING: Plants contain the toxic resin and glycoside wisterin. Most poisonings in recent years are the result of children eating the seeds and pods. Fortunately no deaths have been reported.

SYMPTOMS: Nausea, repeated vomiting, stomach pains, severe diarrhea, dehydration, and collapse.

COMMENTS: Two seeds are believed to be sufficient to cause serious illness in a child. Recovery usually occurs within 24 hours.

YELLOW-OLEANDER Note the long, narrow, leathery leaves; the showy flowers; and odd-shaped fruit (lower center) and seed (lower right) of this deadly shrub or small tree.

Yellow-Oleander, Be-Still Tree

lucky nut *(Thevetia peruviana)*

DESCRIPTION AND DISTRIBUTION: Yellow oleander is a shrub or small tree in the dogbane family with milky juice. Leaves are linear and pointed, simple, entire, alternate, dark green, and glossy. Flowers are tubular, fragrant, and orange or yellow in loose terminal clusters. Fruits (drupes) are triangular and red or yellow, turning black when mature. This attractive plant is introduced from tropical America and is cultivated as an ornamental in the warmer areas of the United States.

TOXIC PARTS: Entire plant, especially the fruit.

POISONING: The plants contain the very toxic cardiac glycosides thevetin and peruvoside which have effects similar to digitalis. One fruit can cause the death of an adult.

SYMPTOMS: Nausea, vomiting, diarrhea, dilated pupils, drowsiness, irregular pulse and heartbeat, high blood pressure, convulsions, and death due to heart failure.

COMMENTS: This plant is considered to be the most frequent cause of human poisonings by plants in Hawaii. Most human deaths occur in native populations using this plant as a medicine. The seeds have been used as a fish poison. The milky sap can cause dermatitis. The stone of the fruit is believed to be a good luck charm.

Yews

ground hemlocks *(Taxus sp.)*

Yews are evergreen trees or large shrubs native to the Northern Hemisphere in higher rainfall belts. The attractive, 2-ranked, dark-green foliage is used extensively throughout the United States in flower wreaths. Leaves, twigs, and seeds of the plants contain the very potent alkaloid taxine which has caused much sickness and sudden death when eaten in quantity. The red fleshy part of the fruit is less toxic and is edible in small quantities.

References

Arena, J. M. 1974. *Poisoning — toxicology, symptoms, treatment.* 3rd ed. Springfield, Il.: American Lecture Ser. Pub. 903.

Arena, J. M. 1974. The peril in plants. *Emergency Medicine* 6(2):221–223, 226–227, 231–232, 234–235, 240–245, 251.

Bailey, L. H. 1951. *Manual of cultivated plants most commonly grown in the continental United States and Canada.* rev. ed. New York: Macmillan.

Bailey, L. H., Bailey, E. Z., and collaborators. 1976. *Hortus third: a concise dictionary of plants cultivated in the United States and Canada.* New York: Macmillan.

Baskin, E. 1967. *The poppy and other deadly plants.* New York: Delacorte Press.

Caldwell, R. L. 1971. "Aflatoxin . . . some problems and progress." *Progr. Agr. in Arizona* 23(2):3, 16.

Ciba-Geigy. Undated. *Plants that poison.* Ardsley, N.Y.: Ciba-Geigy.

Consroe, P. F., and Glow, D. E. 1975. "Clinical toxicology of the desert potato." *Arizona Medicine* 32(6):475–477.

Creekmore, H. 1966. *Daffodils are dangerous: the poisonous plants in your garden.* New York: Walker.

Ellis, M. D., ed. c1975. *Dangerous plants, snakes, arthropods and marine life of Texas.* Galveston, Tx.: U.S. Dept. Health, Education, and Welfare.

Enari, L. 1972. *Poisonous plants of southern California.* Arcadia, Ca.: County of Los Angeles, Dept. Arboreta and Bot. Gardens.

Graf, A. B. 1976. *Exotica, series 3: pictorial encyclopedia of exotic plants from tropical and near-tropic regions.* 8th ed. East Rutherford, N.J.: Roehrs.

Gudas, M. A. 1977. *Poisonous plants: a guide for parents and adventurous eaters.* Phoenix: Do It Now Foundation, Inst. for Chemical Survival.

Hardin, J. W., and Arena, J. M. 1974. *Human poisoning from native and cultivated plants.* Durham, N.C.: Duke Univ. Press.

Harrington, H. D. 1967. *Edible native plants of the Rocky Mountains.* Albuquerque: Univ. New Mexico Press.

Harrington, H. D. 1972. *Western edible wild plants.* Albuquerque: Univ. New Mexico Press.

Jackson, D. F., ed. 1968. *Algae, man, and the environment.* Syracuse, N.Y.: Syracuse Univ. Press.

Kearney, T. H., Pebbles, R. H., and collaborators. 1960. *Arizona flora.* Berkeley: Univ. California Press.

Kelsey, H. P., and Dayton, W. A. 1942. *Standardized plant names.* Harrisburg, Pa.: McFarland.

Kingsbury, J. M. 1964. *Poisonous plants of the United States and Canada.* Englewood Cliffs, N.J.: Prentice-Hall.

Kingsbury, J. M. 1965. *Deadly harvest: a guide to common poisonous plants.* New York: Holt, Rinehart and Winston.

Lampe, K. F., and Fagerstrom, R. 1968. *Plant toxicity and dermatitis: a manual for physicians.* Baltimore, Md.: Williams & Wilkins.

Lincoff, G., and Mitchell, D. H. 1977. *Toxic and hallucinogenic mushroom poisoning: a handbook for physicians and mushroom hunters.* New York: Van Nostrand Reinhold.

Marderosian, A. D. 1966. "Poisonous plants in and around the home." *American J. Pharmaceutical Education* 30:115–140.

Marsh, H. 1974. Urban herbals: common poisonous plants. *Bestways* 2(6):-54–57.

Miller, O. K., Jr. 1972. *Mushrooms of North America.* New York: E. P. Dutton.

Morton, J. F. 1958, 1962. "Ornamental plants with poisonous properties." *Proc. Florida State Hort. Soc.* 71:372–380; 75:484–491.

Morton, J. F. 1977. *Plants poisonous to people in Florida and other warm areas.* 2nd print. Miami, Fl.: Fairchild Tropical Garden.

Muenscher, W. C. 1961. *Poisonous plants of the United States.* New York: Macmillan.

O'Leary, S. B. 1964. "Poisoning in man from eating poisonous plants." *Archives of Environmental Health* 9:216–242.

Schmutz, E. M., Freeman, B. N., and Reed, R. E. 1968. *Livestock-poisoning plants of Arizona.* Tucson: Univ. Arizona Press.

Schultes, R. E. 1976. *Hallucinogenic plants.* New York: Golden Press.

Steger, R. E. 1972. "Native plants poisonous to humans." *J. Range Manage.* 25:71–72. (Reprinted in *Down to Earth* 29(2):18–19. 1973).

Steyn, D. G. 1934. *The toxicology of plants in South Africa together with consideration of poisonous foodstuffs and fungi.* Johannesburg, South Africa: Central News Agency. (Also: *South African Agr. Ser.,* vol. 13).

Stoloff, L. 1977. "Aflatoxins — an overview." p. 7–28. In *Mycotoxins in human and animal health,* Park Forest South, Il.: Pathotox Pub.

Watt, J. M., and Breyer-Brandwijk, M. G. 1962. *The medicinal and poisonous plants of southern and eastern Africa.* London: E. & S. Livingstone, Ltd.

West, E. 1957. *Poisonous plants around the home.* Florida Agr. Exp. Sta. Circ. S-100.

Wiedhopf, R. M., Trumbull, E. R., and Cole, J. R. 1973. "Antitumor agents from *Jatropha macrorhiza* (Euphorbiaceae). I. Isolation and characterization of jatropham." *J. Pharm. Sci.* 62:1206–1207.

Wyeth Laboratories. 1966. *The sinister garden: a guide to the most common poisonous plants*. New York: Wyeth Lab.

Youngken, H. W., Jr., and Karas, J. S. 1964. *Common poisonous plants of New England*. Public Health Service Pub. 1220.

Glossary

Achene a small, dry one-seeded fruit with a thin outer non-splitting covering

Alcohols colorless, volatile, intoxicating liquids and solvents which can depress the nervous system, decrease blood sugar, produce coma, damage the brain, liver, kidney, and intestinal tract, and cause convulsions and death, especially in infants. Plants containing alcohols toxic to humans include snakeroot, jimmyweed, and water-hemlock

Alkaloids complex organic compounds having alkaline (basic) properties and containing nitrogen. Plant alkaloids such as caffeine, nicotine, morphine, cocaine, quinine, and strychnine, are highly poisonous

Alternate the arrangement of leaves along the stem singly at various positions or intervals other than opposite or whorled; the placement of one kind of organ or part at intervals between others

Anaerobic organisms those organisms living or active in the absence of air (free oxygen)

Annual a plant that completes its life cycle and dies in one year or less

Atropine a poisonous white crystalline alkaloid derived from belladonna and related plants. It is used to dilate the pupils of the eye, diminish secretions, relieve pain, and relieve spasms in the stomach, intestines, and rectum

Axil the inner angle where one organ is united with another, especially the inner angle between leaf and stem

Berry a fruit with a fleshy pulp surrounding the seed or seeds

Biennial a plant that lives for two years, producing vegetative growth the first year and usually blooming and fruiting the second year

Bloom in higher plants: to produce or yield flowers; a grayish or powdery coating on fruits or leaves. In algae: an abundant growth of microscopic algal plants drifting on or floating in the water

Bract a reduced or modified leaf usually associated with the flower or seed-head

Bulb an underground bud enveloped with leafy scales or layers

Capsule a dry sack, case, or pod that contains two or more seeds and opens at maturity

cm centimeter; one centimeter equals 0.4 of an inch

Constricted in pods: drawn in or narrowed between the seeds

Cyanide an extremely poisonous white crystalline substance composed of cyanogen gas in combination with some compound or element such as sodium or potassium, and having the odor of bitter almonds

Deciduous plants that shed their leaves at the end of the growing season

Decumbent in botany: stems that trail on the ground and rise at the tips

Depression in medicine: a decrease in vitality or functional activity. In psychology: a normal or pathological condition characterized by discouragement, sadness, inactivity, and feelings of dejection and inadequacy

Dermatitis inflammation of the skin due to exposure to poisons, irritants, or sensitizers. Individuals vary in their sensitivity to hazardous substances

Diarrhea excessively loose and frequent bowel movements

Digitate a compound leaf with the leaflets extended like the fingers of the hand

Drupe a fruit with a fleshy or leathery outer layer over a hard stone which contains the seed

Enlarged in the legend: refers to detail drawings of flowers and fruits, etc., that are enlarged (usually 2 to 10 times) in relation to the rest of the plant.

Entire a continuous smooth margin that is not toothed or divided

Escape a cultivated plant growing wild

Espalier to train a plant to grow flat against a support, such as a wall or trellis; the plant; the support

Evergreen plants that retain some leaves throughout the year

Exserted projecting beyond an enclosing organ or part, as stamens from a corolla

Forb a broad-leafed herbaceous plant

Fronds the leaflike structure in ferns

Fruit the ripened ovary of a plant, including the seed, its envelope, and any closely connected parts

Glabrous having a surface without hairs or projections; smooth

Globose spherical, or nearly so

Glycosides complex compounds that combine a non-sugar group with a sugar, usually glucose. Toxic plant glycosides include cyanides, irritant oils, goiter and blood toxins, and heart stimulants and depressants

Hallucinations perception of imaginary sights, sounds, or objects caused by a disorder of the nervous system or a response to drugs. Most hallucinogenic plants also contain other poisons

Herb an annual or perennial plant that is not woody above ground; one that dies back to the ground each year

Hydrocyanic (prussic) acid a weak, highly poisonous, colorless liquid composed of cyanogen gas in combination with hydrogen, and having the odor of peach blossoms or bitter almonds

Inflorescence   the flower(s) on a stem or flower stalk; the arrangement of the flowers in a cluster

Introduced   a plant species not a part of the original flora of an area

Jaundice   a yellowing of the skin, tissues, and body fluids caused by bile pigments deposited in the blood or tissues

LSD   lysergic acid diethylamide; an organic compound that induces psychotic symptoms (mental disorganization)

m   meter; one meter equals 3.28 feet

Mealy   covered with meal-like (granular) particles; powdery, spotted, or flecked

Narcotic   a drug that induces abnormal drowsiness, dullness of senses, and relief of pain; usually an opiate

Native   a species that is part of the original flora of an area

Naturalized   in reference to plants: an introduced plant that has adapted to an environment to which it is not native

Node   the joint of the stem where the leaf or leaves are attached

Opposite   the positioning of organs in pairs on opposite sides of the same node or flower

Oxalates   salts or esters of oxalic acid that cause corrosion of animal tissues, imbalance in blood chemistry, and precipitation of oxalate crystals in the kidney tubules, which results in failure of the kidneys and urinary tract

Palmate   the shape or arrangement in a leaf where the lobes or veins radiate outwardly from the base like the fingers of a hand

Pappus   a crown of hairs, bristles, awns, or scales

Peptides   organic compounds containing two or more amino acids in which the amino (ammonia) group of one acid is combined with the carboxyl (acid) group of another. If the amino acids are connected in a chain they are polypeptides, in a ring they are cyclopeptides

Perennial   a plant that lives several (usually more than two) years

Petal   one of the inner (usually colored) parts of the flower

Petiole   the stalk of a leaf to which the leaf blade is attached

Phenols   general protoplasmic poisons that can combine with proteins to cause death of nerve endings, capillary damage and paralysis, tissue destruction, gangrene, shock, collapse of heart and blood vessels, kidney damage, and death

Photosensitization   a condition caused by light-reacting substances in the bloodstream that come directly from plants eaten or from normal digestion products no longer eliminated because of liver dysfunction. Effects include eruptions on light-colored skin after exposure to sunlight, secondary bacterial infection, shock, and liver damage

Phytotoxins   complex vegetable proteins of high toxicity that act as antigens causing an antibody reaction in animals when eaten; also called toxalbumins

Pinnate   a compound leaf with the leaflets arranged singly or in rows on opposite sides of a common stalk or petiole; the veins of a leaf arranged in rows on opposite sides of the central vein like the barb divisions of a feather

Poison   a substance, usually a drug, that impairs, injures, or kills an organism through chemical action

Polyploid   the condition of having more than twice the number of basic (monoploid) chromosome numbers

Pome   a fleshy fruit, such as an apple, containing a core and two-to-several seeds

Resins   complex virulent compounds varying widely in chemistry that affect nervous and muscular tissues; also called resinoids

Rootstock   an underground stem (with nodes and scaly leaves) that may produce green shoots on the upper side of the nodes and roots below

Saponins   certain plant glycosides which form colloidal solutions and produce a nonalkaline soapy lather when shaken in water. In combination with an irritant they can cause the destruction of red blood cells in animals

Seed   the ripened ovule that contains the embryo capable of forming a new plant

Sepal   one of the outer (usually green) parts of the flower

Sessile   a condition in which the plant part lacks a stalk, such as a leaf without a petiole

Shrubs   relatively low-growing, much-branched, and many-stemmed woody perennials

Simple   undivided leaves or unbranched stems

Spore   a reproductive cell of ferns and other non-flowering plants

Stamen   the male or pollen-producing organ in flowering plants

Succulent   fleshy, thick, and juicy

Tendril   a slender coiling branch or modified leaf with which plants attach themselves to other plants or objects

230

Tooth   a small lobe or point on the margin of a leaf or other organ

Toxic principle   a chemical agent that produces a toxic or poisonous reaction in animals

Toxin   a poisonous unstable colloidal proteinaceous substance produced by plants or animals which affects the metabolic activities of a living organism; typically, one capable of inducing antibody formation

Tree   a large woody plant more than 3 m (10 feet) tall and usually with a single bole or trunk below the branches

Tubers   a thickened underground stem, such as a potato, bearing buds and containing stored food

Weed   any unwanted, usually undesirable, plant — whether grass, forb, shrub, or tree

Whorl   a ring of three or more similar organs, such as leaves, at the same node

Index

233

234

235